Plain English for Cops

Plain English for Cops

Nicholas Meier
R.J. Adams

Carolina Academic Press
Durham, North Carolina

ISBN 0-89089-846-4
LCCN 99-066963

Carolina Academic Press
700 Kent Street
Durham, NC 27701
Telephone (919) 489-7486
Fax (919) 493-5668
E-mail: cap@cap-press.com
www.cap-press.com

Printed in the United States of America

Without the support and encouragement of our families, we could not have completed this book. We dedicate it to them: Julia, Kathleen, Betsy, Kat, Hannah, and Molly.

Contents

Foreword

The Importance of Police Report Writing Skills

Isaiah McKinnon, Ph.D.
Chief of Police (Ret.), City of Detroit

When we think about the types of skills police officers need in order to perform their jobs well, we usually think in terms of defensive tactics, proficiency in the use of firearms, and pursuit driving. Often, we overlook the importance of developing the skills associated with preparing high quality police reports. The ability to prepare an accurate and concise police report is a basic but crucial aspect of a police officer's job. Report writing is a constant fact of life for law enforcement. Reports, memos, updates, evaluations—all of these and more have to be written to drive the information machine that is law enforcement.

Unfortunately, a great deal of law enforcement writing is mired in stilted language, unclear reporting, inconsistencies and mistakes, jargon and inappropriate word choice. This directly impacts how the justice system works. Dependent on information, the justice system will run more efficiently and effectively when law enforcement reports are clear, concise, and accurate. Due to the importance of writing in the American justice system, it is vital that law enforcement writing is upgraded so that reports help, instead of hinder, the system.

Well-written reports make everyone's job easier. The police supervisor is satisfied that everything is accounted for and doesn't need more information. The prosecutor who reads the report understands everything and doesn't have to conduct additional interviews.

Without a doubt, we as professional police officers are morally obligated to provide the public with the best possible police service. The wheels of justice spin more smoothly when police reports are written accurately, clearly, and concisely.

Preface

Police report writing has often been compared to having a root canal done without the benefit of Novocain™. This book is the Novocain™. While we can't make you love to write reports, we can make writing a good report far less painful. From patrol officers to chiefs, report writing is a common lament with each level of the hierarchy having its own perspective. The patrol officer may sincerely believe that most of the reports she authors will go nowhere but the file and acts accordingly. The chief, on the other hand, may see these reports as the basis for planning, staffing, budgeting, or the first line of defense against complaints lodged against the officer or the department. No matter what your perspective, do not underestimate the importance of report writing to your profession. We think Steven Walker, a parole supervisor for the Michigan Department of Corrections, said it best: **"It's more than writing; it's making things work."**

One of the major advantages of our book is its simplicity. This book, unlike most of the textbooks available for police report writing, is reality based. We recognize that report formats* vary from agency to agency. Rather than focus on the report formats of any one or two departments, we will provide generic elements of report design as we concentrate on conveying information in an honest, clear, concise, and complete manner. This book will assist the writer of any police communication in understanding the importance of clear writing from a global perspective, not just from the limited point of view of any single department or officer. We purposely avoid lengthy discussions of report formats since we recognize that each department has its own preferences, and therefore

---

*Throughout this book, we use the word **report** to mean any document written by a member of a law enforcement agency. Reports include, but are not limited to, field reports. The techniques and concepts that allow you to produce a well-written field report will allow you to produce well-written memos, budget reports, leave requests, requests for transfers and any other professional document you may be called upon to write. We use the word **format** to refer to the physical arrangement of the report on the page, how it looks on paper.

an attempt to address each department's style would be futile. Use of your local agency's forms and formats in completing the exercises provided is encouraged.

We have attempted to organize this book into broad, and we hope somewhat humorous, themes based on our analysis of hundreds of police reports from departments ranging in size from three to one-thousand employees. We are convinced that police writers continue to make basic mistakes that can have a devastating effect on their credibility and that of their department. These common, relatively simple errors seem to be universal in police writing. You will learn from the mistakes of others, and this knowledge can be applied to your writing in the field.

This is not an ivory tower book. All examples are real; none were fabricated from our positions as "chairborne rangers." Only the identifying information has been changed at the request of the departments who cooperated in this project. We avoided using examples from high-profile, media-sensationalized cases because the focus should be on the writing, not the case. Instead, we focused on the work of the typical officer—the world of routine, mundane, day-to-day documentation. As you read and work through the examples, keep in mind that most were approved by at least one supervisor and, in many cases, by others in the chain of command.

This book was originally planned for use as a primary textbook in a college course or police academy. As it evolved, we became convinced that it is also useful as a tool for Field Training Officers in preparing the new officer for independence and for supervisors in remediating officers who are having difficulty with written communication. It can also be used as part of a comprehensive inservice training program.

Officers often feel that their reports go nowhere and are read by no one. A unique aspect of this book is the inclusion of focus boxes which we have titled "From the ...." Contributors to these focus boxes are representative of the many professionals who depend on quality reports to do their jobs. You will learn to appreciate the importance of your documentation from the insights of criminal justice professionals: prosecutors, chiefs, supervisors, defense attorneys, the news media, and others.

Even the most poorly written police report can be transformed if the officer keeps a few basic concepts in mind. It's usually a simple fix. To that end, we will focus on the KISS (Keep It Simple, Stupid) method.

To the Instructor

Typically police skills are not taught by demonstrating incorrect methods. For example, you do not demonstrate improper baton use by simulating striking the suspect over the head and urging your students not to do so. In a stressful situation, the officer will resort to the most dramatic examples that she learned during training. Thus, we demonstrate only the correct way to use a baton. However, using examples of mistakes in the report writing process and the corresponding humor found in these mistakes can create memory pegs that the officer can remember and apply when she is writing her report.

We have to face the reality that most officers did not enter law enforcement because of their love for report writing. If you are using this text in the basic training/college setting, we suspect your students, while interested in the topic, really can't wait to get into the "real" police training. If you are teaching an inservice training program, be prepared for empty front rows, full back rows, lots of eye rolling, contemplation of the ceiling, and other signs of interest. If you are working with an officer who has been sent to you for individual remediation, be prepared for resistance. In each case, YOU are going to have to generate interest. We have found there are some ways to do that. First and foremost, DON'T teach a traditional grammar class. Don't lecture on nouns, future perfect verbs, and modal auxiliaries. Use examples from local police agencies. If you are teaching an inservice, use copies of your departmental reports as a tool to get your officers to buy into the training as our first Focus Box clearly illustrates.

From the Assistant Prosecutor*

I recently trained all road officers and supervising sergeants in the Lansing Police Department regarding domestic assault report

---

* Alice Phillips is an Assistant Prosecuting Attorney with Ingham County, Michigan. She specializes in domestic violence cases.

writing techniques. A mock domestic assault scene was staged, and two officers were asked to interview the witnesses. All officers were then asked what they would list in their report (based on the statements provided) and what the Prosecutor would need to successfully prosecute the case. After hearing their comments, the officers were provided with three well-written domestic assault police reports and three poorly written domestic assault reports (these were retyped and names/addresses changed). The officers were broken into groups of six (with each group covering one report) and were asked to present the good and bad points of the report to the class (focusing primarily on whether the statutory requirements were met). The officers evaluating the three poorly written reports were astonished that such reports existed. When I held up the actual reports and indicated the reports had been produced by three of their fellow officers, they were appalled. They clearly understood at that point the importance of each police report in proceeding with victimless prosecution in domestic assault situations.

We have selected examples for both their humor and tragedy. We have specifically omitted any answer keys since there is no one correct way to write or rewrite the exercises. Agencies differ in their approaches; therefore, we encourage you to complete the exercises yourself. This will allow you to tailor your answers to your jurisdiction and your teaching to your audience, i.e., academy, inservice, trainee, etc. Convey to your students that report writing is more than just slot-filling. Have them struggle with the answers. The only way to write well is by writing again, and again, and again. Encourage the use of small group work, moot court exercises, and peer evaluations. Take the sample reports provided and have students rewrite each report based on the information given. Compare what each student writes to see the wide variety of factual interpretations. You can also use your own "uglies" (a term we use to refer to reports that are worse than bad) as a basis for training.

Throughout this book we dismiss certain rules of grammar, offer some broad generalizations, avoid discussions of some of the more technical aspects of writing, and in general play a little fast and loose with the elements of style. We are sure that you will be able to find exceptions to the rules we offer here. So can we.

A technical table of contents is included at the end of this book for those of you who want to know where traditional grammar concepts fit into each chapter. For those of you who wish to make a detailed analysis of the exceptions, modifications, etc., feel free to refer to Quirk and Greenbaum's treatise. But remember, our purpose is not to burden the officer with a traditional grammar text, rather it is to provide the officer with a roadmap to aid in the preparation of documents that are clear and complete.

To the Officer

We use the term officer throughout this book. If you are a student beginning your career in law enforcement, we want you to think of yourself not as a student, but as a police officer. We want you to approach report writing as you would any other aspect of your training: survival. The impact of a poorly written report can be as devastating as taking a bullet. Either can end your career. If you are an experienced officer who has been selected as a person who can benefit from this book — take heart! You will be able to relate to most of our examples because you have been there. Use the experiences of your fellow officers from around the country and improve your own abilities.

We use the *Mary Poppins* approach to police writing: humor is our spoonful of sugar. Just as firearms, driving, defensive tactics, investigative skills, and patrol tactics improve with practice and experience, so will your report writing. You might actually come to enjoy the challenge of completing a report that you will be proud of. You will become known by your reports. Poor reports, poor reputation; great reports, great reputation.

From the FTO Supervisor*

Seventeen years ago, as a wide-eyed rookie, I was treated to a lesson about the importance of report writing by a veteran police officer at the same time as a group of elementary school students. This lesson occurred at a career day at a local elementary school. The veteran officer asked the children what the most important tool was for a police officer. We heard many of the responses that I myself was thinking: gun, handcuffs, and police car. To each and every answer the veteran officer replied, "No" until the

---

*Sgt. Paul Erlandson is with the Township of Kalamazoo (MI) Police Department. He is an expert in traffic accident reconstruction.

answers dried up. The officer then reached into his pocket, pulled out a pen, and told the students that the pen was absolutely the most important tool for a police officer. He explained to the students how the pen was most important to the police officer for report writing.

Seventeen years later, that tool may have changed to a tape recorder, personal computer, or laptop computer, but the end result is no less important today. As a sergeant and Field Training Supervisor, I review a multitude of police reports, directives, memos, and teletypes. There is nothing that will cause more consternation, joke making at the expense of the author, or just plain incredulity than a poorly written document. As police officers, we are judged most often by the written report or the memo.

I have told many trainees and veteran officers that the greatest job can be undermined by a poorly written report. Using cliches and stilted phrases, failing to include the necessary elements, and failing to use proper grammar reduce the most impressive job to a poor piece of work. A well-written report will save you from unnecessary court time and from civil suits. We must learn to write clearly, concisely, and properly. I have seen many highly talented applicants not be considered further for employment because of their inability to write. I have also seen many highly talented veteran officers be joked about or fail to get an arrest warrant issued because of a poorly written report. As police officers we have to be able to express ourselves by the written word.

Acknowledgments

This book would not have been possible without the support of many people. We are indebted to those named here as well as those who wish to remain anonymous.

We would like to thank the following people who contributed source material to us, who supported us with critical comments throughout this project, or who spent countless hours reviewing the manuscript and providing important insights: Sgt.Gail Barnes, Detroit Police Department; R. Danvers Child; Assistant Director James Conser, Ohio Peace Officer's Training Academy; Det. Carol Dedow, Western Michigan University Department of Public Safety; Michael Deppe (Ret.), Lake Station (IN) Police Department and Chaplain FOP Lodge 153; Sgt. Paul Erlandson, Township of Kalamazoo (MI) Police Department; Det. Jan Erlandson, Kent County (MI) Sheriff's Department; Sgt. Dan Frever, Kalamazoo (MI) Sheriff's Department; Pam Gwilliams, Portage (MI) Police Department; Det. Ken Holmes, Maricopa County (AZ) Sheriff's Office; Deputy Chief Mike Jungel, Portage (MI) Police Department; Lt. Dan Lind, Grand Rapids (MI) Police Department; Capt. Jeff Maggers, Jefferson County (KY) Sheriff's Department; Lt. Kenneth Montgomery, Detroit Police Department; Steven Walker, Parole Supervisor, Michigan Department of Corrections; Administrator Joseph Leary, Van Buren County (MI) Juvenile Court; Ronald Adams; Off. Jack Bogema, Portage (MI) Police Department; Patricia A. Roder; Prof. Susan Hollar, Kalamazoo Valley Community College; Prof. Susan Townsend, Kalamazoo Valley Community College; Dean Dick Roder, Kalamazoo Valley Community College; Prof. Rick Brill, Kalamazoo Valley Community College; Prof. Patty Cherpas, Kalamazoo Valley Community College; Off. Charles Dahlinger, Kalamazoo (MI) Department of Public Safety and the Director of In-Service Training at Kalamazoo Valley Community College; Prof. John Holmes, Kalamazoo Valley Community College; Prof. Bill Lay, Kalamazoo Valley Community College; and Dean Alfred Sagar, Kalamazoo Valley Community College.

Literally hundreds of hours were spent building a data base of report errors to use in this book. The following criminal justice students were pivotal in the input of data as well as providing feedback to us as the project progressed: Brent Dontje, Craig Jackson, Lisa Oberheu, Donald R. Peek, Greg Smith, Jennifer VanSchaemelhout, Kelly Winfrey and Natalie Wood.

We would like to thank those professionals in the criminal justice system who took the time to give their insights on the importance of the report writing process. These contributors were not only the source for our Focus Boxes, they were an inspiration to us in the development of this book. They are truly appreciated. Undersheriff Michael Anderson, Kalamazoo County (MI) Sheriff's Department; Lt. C. Lee Bennett, Springfield (MA) Police Department; Prof. Ron Bretz, Thomas M. Cooley Law School; Lt. Helen Cooper (Ret.), Chatenooga (TN) Police Department; Prof. Timothy Dees, Floyd College; Stuart Dunnings III, Prosecutor, Ingham County (MI); Chief Edward P. Edwardson, Wyoming (MI) Police Department; Loren Goldfarb; Chief Isiah McKinnon (Ret.), Detroit Police Department; Alice Phillips, Assistant Prosecutor, Ingham County (MI); Prof. Darrell Ross, East Carolina University; Off. Brad Schutter, Wyoming (MI) Police Department; and Sgt. Geoff Sjostrom, Oak Park (IL) Police Department.

We would like to recognize two very talented police trainees: Nathan Carr, whose original oil painting was created specifically for this book; and, Anne C. Yingling, whose cover design incorporated Nate's painting. Also, a very special thanks to Dave Coverly for his generous permission to use "Speed Bump" and to John R. Koslek III of *Koz Art* in Kalamazoo for his original illustrations, using Corel Draw™, which appear throughout the book.

Finally, we would like to thank the following members of our Basic Police Training classes who provided valuable insight to this book from the trainee's perspective: Stuart R. Bell III, Kevin A. Callahan, Nathan Carr, Brian Gard, William L. Greene, Nathan Lutz, Matthew May, Frederick A. Milton, Jr., Marvin G. Petty, Matthew C. Shepard, Dwight A. Stallard, Heather Wolkow, Mike Wordelman, and Anne C. Yingling.

Plain English for Cops

Chapter 1

WIIFM

We have spent literally thousands of hours in classrooms, seminar rooms, and training sessions as both students and instructors. If you are like us, our classmates, and our students, right about now you have to be asking yourself, "What's In It For Me?" What's in it for you can be summed up in one word: Survival. Whether it is winning the fierce competition for a job, graduating from the academy, completing your field training, getting promoted, surviving direct- and cross-examination, or protecting yourself and your department from damaging litigation, there is a common thread, and that is writing skill.

> **From the Street Cop***
>
> Most new cops think that the skills that will allow them to fight crime are the more spectacular ones — athletic skill, driving skill, shooting skill, interrogation skill. And, in fact, those skills might help you "catch" crooks, but they don't help as much to convict them. This is where report writing skills come in.

As our Street Cop says, report writing is central to doing any task well. Want to get a job? Write well. Want to complete your probationary period? Write well. Want to get promoted? Write well. Want to look good in a court room? Write well. Want to look like a jack-ass? Write good.

---

* Timothy Dees is a former police officer, FTO, and sergeant. He is currently a professor at Floyd College in Georgia.

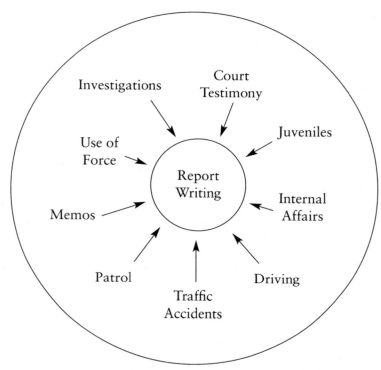

Report Writing is Central to Doing Any Task Well

If you look at report writing and other forms of documentation from a survival perspective, what you write will have a major impact on your life. Many administrators will make the decision to interview you based on how you look on paper. You might have the greatest potential for a police career, but your application will go in the circular file because of minor editing errors, misspellings, and so forth. Would you arrange to interview this officer if this application came across your desk?

"I am in seek of a position as an officer of the law."

You might be the best cop out there, but if you can't write well, you simply cannot function adequately as a police officer.

From the Administrative Assistant to the Chief*

Cover Letters

Content: Keep cover letters brief and to the point.

Accuracy: Call the agency and request the name of the Chief and the individual responsible for the applications. I've received letters addressed to our previous Chief and "To whom it may concern" and "Police Department."

Most cover letters are acceptable and are pooled with the other hundreds of applicants. However, the goal is to distinguish yourself from the others. The "outstanding" letters reflect an accepted form layout, are generated by a word processing program and

---

* Officer Brad Schutter is currently with the Wyoming (MI) Police Department. He has a Master's Degree in Criminal Justice from Michigan State University.

quality printer, and are printed on high quality paper. They are addressed to the appropriate person.

Distinguish yourself!

Take a look at the following narrative written by an experienced officer.

Officer Jackson whent to the Smith resdence because sombody vandelized there mailbox. Unknow partys placed what appeared to be a cherrybom and blowed the sideof the box out. The Smiths beleave the partys next door our involved. Officer Jackson talked to the partys and they denyed the allegasion. Off. beleaves theres a ongoin neighberhood problem and this could be retalization.

Was he functionally illiterate, tired, rushed, or did he just not care? What was this officer trying to communicate? How does it reflect on the department? The officer? Does it slow you down when you read it? Can you do a better job? Correct the narrative. Compare your corrections with those of a fellow officer. Were your corrections the same?

There are a few sadistic supervisors who take great pleasure in shaming their subordinates when it comes to proper documentation. One supervisor, whom we refer to as Sergeant DeSade, gleefully told us how, upon receiving a report with multiple errors, he would inform the officer over the radio for all to hear that the report was unacceptable. The officer would have to return to the station to correct a single error in the report. Sergeant DeSade would repeat the process for each error, waiting until the officer had resumed patrol before recalling the officer again. While, fortunately, most supervisors are not like Sgt. DeSade, it is still no fun to have your reports kicked back by a supervisor or a report review unit.

Memorandums are another important type of report.

From the Administrative Assistant to the Chief

Memos often reflect a tremendous amount of personal information about you. You may reveal direct and/or indirect signals of your skill level, academic achievement, area of expertise, and feelings or emotions.

The most disturbing memos are ones which are personal (Jim is a jerk, and I don't like working for him), contain profanity, use cliches (over my dead body), and analogies (it was big as a house). Do not personalize the topic or issue because it will be clearly evident in your memo!

Memos should provide the reader with a direct, objective and complete understanding of the topic or issue. Provide personal feelings during a private conversation with the reader.

Read the following memorandum from an officer who became ill on duty and was unable to complete the shift. Is this memo a positive reflection on the officer? Is this memo a positive reflection on the department? Did the officer conclude the writing process by proofreading? Would you have approved this memorandum as the officer's lieutenant did?

"I am unable to continue my tour of duty due to the medicine I took prior to work. I was Niqul day time. I has made me dizzy and has given my stomach cramps. Also I has given me a "high" feeling with I do not think safe to be working."

[Signed by officer, approved by lieutenant]

Can you repair this memorandum?

Regardless of the grammatical and mechanical shortcomings of our "NyQuilled" officer, at least he was honest, the foundation of all police communications.

From the Undersheriff*

The Truth Shall Not be Slanted

---

* Michael Anderson is currently Undersheriff at the Kalamazoo County (MI) Sheriff's Department. Prior to joining KCSD, he was with the Michigan State Police for 23 years retiring as a Major in Charge of the Uniformed Services Division.

Absolute integrity needs to be continuously demonstrated in all facets of police work. My thirty-five years in law enforcement have convinced me that only a very few officers would ever fail any integrity litmus test placed in front of them except perhaps in one arena. Unfortunately, I believe more than a few officers succumb to an integrity problem I call "slanted" report writing. Perhaps something as simple as writing a synopsis of an interview with a witness who doesn't concur with every detail of what a half dozen other witnesses said will end up in a report appearing the same as the other witnesses or even worse, the witness is left out of the report altogether in the belief that he/she isn't credible. By my definition, this is slanted report writing because the report has been deliberately or subconsciously slanted in the direction we want it to go as opposed to having a direction of its own. Reporting the "whole truth" must be the objective of any investigator. Anything less may cause the entire criminal justice system to ignore the obvious.

Your documentation must be brutally honest. You cannot leave anything out, whether or not you think it hurts your case. We never like to put ourselves in a bad light, and we don't like to leave any "gaps" in our case. In psychology, it's called the law of closure. Fancy words for a desire to have no loose ends. However, if you tie up those loose ends by using a little creative fiction, you will suffer. At a minimum, you will be disciplined; at a maximum, you will be sentenced. Ask yourself if you would like to be in the position of this officer who "fudged" a report about why he failed to respond to a radio call. Did this officer violate the undersheriff's first commandment? You bet he did. As a result, he had to write the following memo to the Internal Affairs Unit:

Sir,

I am writing about the incident that happened on August 21, 1998. On that particular night I did not answer my radio do to the fact that I fell asleep. On that day I was taking care of my daughter and didn't get to sleep. It's not an excuse, it's just what happened.

That night I was working by myself in District 6. Detective Schwartz was the one that told me that they was calling me on the radio. Lt. Harrington gave me supervisors check and ask me what happened. I told him that I must have turned the radio off by mistake. He told me that Lt. Yoder wanted a special [memorandum] by the end of the shift which I did turn in with that same story.

Now to make this thing clear. Taking the advise of a certain officer I didn't say that I fell asleep. I said something else. That certain officer got a case amnesia when interviewed by I.I.U. [Internal Investigations Unit] Now to look back at the situation, I should have just told the truth from get go.

Also, I didn't fall asleep on purpose. I had a terrible headache and I was very tired and I didn't want to drive like that so all I wanted to do is take a break for 10-15 minutes before I went back on the road. If I really wanted to fall asleep all I had to do is hook up with another car that way I didn't have to worry about missing a call.

Officer Post

The written word can be used internally (as above) or externally. Police reports are legal documents. They are often the only record of your action — good or bad. They can support you as a witness for the prosecution or as a defendant in a lawsuit. And let's face it, lawsuits are a growing concern. Whether or not you get to experience the joy of a civil action will often depend on the quality of your report.

From the Trainer*

Recently, I was visited by an attorney for a woman who had been injured during an arrest. It seems that there was some type of argument at the scene of a traffic stop. As a result, the woman suffered a broken leg. This particular attorney was trying to determine whether or not to file suit and sought some information from me regarding documentation in a use of force situation.

---

* From an experience of one of the authors.

When I looked at the report, I was dumbfounded. There was no information about any use of force. No documentation of what type of resistance was encountered and what type of force was used. No documentation regarding escalation or de-escalation. No indication that the woman suffered any injuries or whether or not she was treated. No justification for the use of force. Was the use of force justified? I suspected it was, because I knew who trained the officer. Further, I also knew that the officer had to know the importance of documentation or she would never have graduated from the academy. Yet, for whatever reason, the use of force became indefensible because the report was incomplete. The department settled out of court for $25,000, $25,000 that the department could have saved if the officer had spent an additional thirty minutes documenting the incident.

It has been said that bad cases make bad law. Bad reports make for bad cases.

From the Use of Force Expert Witness*

It is highly likely that a civil case will be brought against an officer when various forms of force are used in effecting an arrest. Allegations of excessive force can be lodged whether the citizen sustained an injury or not and whether or not the officer followed proper procedures. The first line of defense against a civil lawsuit for allegations of excessive force is the officer's written report. A carefully drafted use of force report is as important as making the decision to use a level of force at the time of the arrest. As an expert witness who is retained to defend the officer's action in a particular arrest, the first document I review as part of the complete file is the officer's written report. The second document I review is the police department's use of force policy, and I cross check the report against the policy. An officer's choice in utilizing a level of force must be made in accordance with the current

* Darrell Ross is a nationally recognized expert witness in the use of force, the Director of Research for Pressure Point Control Tactics, and is a Professor of Criminal Justice at East Carolina University.

status of the law, within the boundaries of departmental policy, and within the scope of the circumstances of the arrest environment. Therefore, the reporting officer must thoroughly articulate his or her involvement in the incident to justify the decision to use force. Moreover, the plaintiff's lawyer will retain a police expert to analyze the named officer's report in a civil lawsuit to determine whether force was utilized reasonably. The police expert for the plaintiff will review the report with a highly critical eye, looking for weaknesses, incompleteness, and any ambiguities which may exist. The plaintiff's attorney will examine the report with microscopic detail in order to discover inaccuracies in hopes of strengthening the case for allegations of excessive force.

The yesteryear adage of "less is best" does not apply today. Police use of force reports that only contain: "I was dispatched to 123 Easy Street, went to arrest the subject and he fought with me, I was able to control and handcuff him, and later transported him to the county jail," just do not suffice, particularly when the individual is sitting in court with a brace around his neck. Officers who write reports in this fashion, believing they can fill in the gaps during a deposition or through court testimony are sadly mistaken and are asking for considerable grief. As an expert witness in this field I would be inclined to refuse a case where an officer did not fully detail his or her involvement in the incident, thinking the officer may be attempting to cover up behavior that is missing in the report.

Thorough reports are not conceived by chance but require practice and careful deliberation on the part of the officer.

What's in it for you? Career survival.

Exercise: Text Hunt

If you don't know why *Mary Poppins* is important to this book, you need this exercise. Most of us tend to jump into the learning process without getting the big picture. If you want to travel from Ottumwa, Iowa, to Honolulu, Hawaii, do you hop in the car and start driving? No, you get a road map (and perhaps a small boat). You need to see the big picture. Before jumping into the remaining chapters, you should get a feel for the book as a whole rather than looking at each chapter individually. Text Hunt is designed to let you see the big picture. So, grab a cup of coffee and a donut* and let's get started.

Text Hunt

1.   Sometimes a book has more than one author. How many people collaborated on writing the text?
2.   Name the author(s) of the text.
3.   Books are published by many different publishing companies or "houses." Who published this text book ? In what state?
4.   What year was this text published?
5.   What were the chief's three commandments?
6.   What is the section called that lists the authors' credits in the front of the book?
7.   Who wrote the *Foreword*?
8.   What is ASCOT?
9.   What is the *Mary Poppins* approach?
10. What is GTSOBOMHRN?
11. What is the KISS method?
12. Is there a situation in which the title to Chapter 5 could be correct?
13. What can a squirrel do?
14. What does the acronym PRELIMINARY mean?
15. What is the difference between *report* and *format*?
16. What is the word on the street? What does it mean?
17. How many traffic signs are in this text?
18. What is a major problem with using the *10 Code* in your report?
19. What can't a squirrel do?
20. Why would you have to connect the dots? Where is the solution?

---

* Or, as one of our reviewer's suggested, "A bagel, it's the 90s."

Chapter 2

Out of the Station and Into the Real World

Shakespeare was right, "All the world is a stage, and the cops are but players upon it." O.K., so he didn't really say that, and we apologize for playing fast and loose with his work. But it is true; cops are always playing to an audience. Shakespeare truly understood his audience and wrote accordingly. You need to understand your audience and what they want from your report and then, like Shakespeare, write your report according to their needs. To make the task difficult, your audience, like a theater audience, is varied and consists entirely of critics. To make the task even more difficult, every member of your audience has a separate agenda. To make the task seem impossible, you must satisfy everyone with a single document. Impossible? No. Difficult? Yes. Easy? With practice.

You have been exposed to many technical documents which were not written with a diverse audience in mind. Look at your state's penal code. Look at the documents that came with your computer or VCR. Did you need a phraseology guide to understand the penal code? Did you need *DOS for Dummies* to understand your computer? Is your VCR still flashing 12:00? If you answered yes to any of these questions, you have been abused by a writer who lacked audience awareness. When YOU write, consider your audience and don't subject them to the abuses you have suffered.

Police documents, like all GOOD technical documents, are meant to be used by someone, and as we saw in WIIFM, your writing is not limited to use by someone in your department only. Recognizing this will save you from embarrassment. You must begin with an awareness of who the end users of your report are. Then, you must recognize what they need from your report to do their jobs. If you do this, your report is not the end product of one event; it is a vital link in an entire chain of events. If you tend to doubt the importance of your report as a vital link, the insight of a couple of players in the system might shed some light on the issue:

13

From the Prosecutor*

Details, details, details! The success of the Prosecutor depends directly on the police officers involved at the scene, the investigation that is performed and the reports that are prepared. Since the Prosecutor is traditionally not present at the crime scene, the police report is the only opportunity for the prosecutor to fully understand what occurred before, during and after the commission of the crime. Officers must provide enough detail in their report so that the Prosecutor can visualize what occurred.

From the Public Defender**

Make no mistake—the police report is the first important source of information for a defense attorney in a criminal case. If possible, most attorneys will review the available police reports before meeting with the client. The reason for this is simple—it is always helpful to have an idea of the case against your client before the client gives you his or her version. Thus, the police report is a critical document, the first critical document the attorney is likely to encounter.

Opposite sides, same goals. Becoming aware of your audience's needs requires you to think in terms of a global perspective. You need to rethink your approach to writing reports and where those reports fit into the entire criminal justice system. The exercise on the next page illustrates what we mean. The eight perimeter dots outline your routine work space. Connect the nine dots by using four straight lines. Your pen may not leave the paper.

---

* Stuart Dunning III is currently the Ingham County (MI) Prosecutor.
** Ronald Bretz is Professor of Law at the Thomas Cooley Law School. Prior to joining the Cooley Faculty, he was with the Michigan State Appellate Defender's Office.

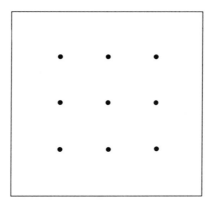

It cannot be done unless you expand your perspective and go outside the artificial limitations the dots seem to impose. Keep in mind that your document has many uses outside the self-imposed limitations you discovered above.

Whether you are writing a memo, a letter, an internal report, or a field report, you know that good documents begin with good notes. Who is the audience of your notes? First and foremost, you are. The first critic who needs to be satisfied is you.

You were taught that upon arriving at the scene of an incident, you must answer the who, what, when, where, why, and how in order to generate your field notes. Your field notes will be full of abbreviations and cop shorthand. This is an important skill to develop. It saves time and increases your investigative efficiency. However, be careful to use only generally accepted, standardized abbreviations in your field notes. If you are an investigator, keep in mind that you might have another member of the audience who will rely on your notes: the follow-up investigator. As you begin to develop your own style and shorthand, keep a list of your personal abbreviations in the event that a second person must take up the case after you are transferred or leave the department. But remember, abbreviations have their place in your field notes, not in your final document. Your field notes are a journal of your activities over time and follow no particular sequence of events. Field notes are chaotic, scattered, fragmented thoughts and random bits of information. You put them together to make a complete and accurate picture. However, to complete the picture, you need all the pieces.

Sample Field Notes

Several methods for field note taking have been developed over the years. Some are well known while others are unique to a particular jurisdiction. They all share one common trait. They provide you with a guide to insure that you obtain all the information necessary to create a well-written report. Your notes are the pieces of a puzzle, and your final report is a complete and accurate picture. It is not our intent to discuss field note taking methods in great detail here. You will learn or have learned all of the essential elements of field note taking elsewhere in your training. There is, though, a distinct difference between field notes and your report. Remember that YOU are the primary audience of your field notes, while your reports have a diverse audience.

BEETLE BAILEY

Reprinted with Special Permission of King Features Syndicate

Once you have answered the who, what, when, where, why, and how of the incident, you need to ask yourself the who, what, when, where, why, and how of the audience. When you take up your clipboard, computer, typewriter, or tape recorder, you should take care to insure that your report contains all the facts, BUT you also need to anticipate your audience and answer these same questions—Who will read it? What are they looking for? When will they read it? Where will they read it? Why do they want to read it? How are they going to use it, and quite possibly, to whom will they "apply" the information? Difficult to do at 3:00 a.m. under a dome light or on the telephone while your adrenaline is pumping. What if you can't identify the person to whom your report will be sent? In that case, write to the office, not the person. You may not know the coroner, but you do know that the coroner's office will read the report. Write accordingly.

As you noticed during Text Hunt, we use focus boxes to show just how many different people use your reports. Because of this diverse audience, your report should have only one interpretation, one that is completely factual and legal. Your goal is to generate a document that can be interpreted only one way.

From the Street Cop

"Officer Brown shot Jones running out the door." Who was running: Brown or Jones? If you make an unclear statement that can be taken in a way other than the one you intended, it will weaken your case. It isn't all that difficult to edit out these errors, but it does take time and attention to detail that many officers don't bother with. That attention to detail is one of the things that separates mediocre officers from great ones.

Ask yourself: To What Audience Were These Officers Writing?

"Writers given to P/R's to 307 Main on man shot from dispatch." (Writing to the file cabinet)

"Instantaneously, the suspect waived the weapon in Officer Smith's path and that of myself, and I took ready, aim, to fire on him." (Writing to Lawyers)

"Wrts Made the above loc obs the above perp whom stated he was the driver of the below listed impounded veh highly intoxacated." (Writing to other officers)

But what about the report that you know is going nowhere? What should you care? It's only going into storage. WIIFM? There are two very good WIIFMs. First, police reports are forever.

From the Street Cop

Police reports are forever.

The great foot pursuit or free-for-all at the downtown bar will be relived the next day at roll call, and maybe even for weeks afterward, but those things are eventually forgotten. However, the worst report you ever write will never die, and can always come back to haunt you. These things sit in files, or microfilm, or on hard drives, and can be brought back years later, even after you have forgotten about them. It is said that old cops never die; their reports don't, either.

You never know where your reports will go.

Second, you are how you train. If you are sloppy in what appears to be insignificant, you will be sloppy in the significant. Keep in mind that practice doesn't make perfect. Perfect practice makes perfect. For years, officers dumped spent casings from their revolvers into their hands and put them in their pockets because it saved time in policing up the range. All that changed after an incident in which officers who were killed during a firefight were found with spent casings in their pockets. Valuable time to protect themselves was lost because of habits developed during hours on the range. FBI agents died during a firefight in Miami while their body armor remained in their cars. While about 20% of all officer fatalities occur during unknown risk traffic stops, officers continue to be complacent and to make bad approaches.

Do you still doubt the significance of even the most insignificant report? If your answer is yes...

Where do you think we got all of our examples for this book?

Application 1

Just how many people may read your report? There are 8 documents listed below. For each type of document, list the different people who might logically have to or need to read it to do their jobs.

Employment application   Burglar alarm call
Academy memo   Homicide report
Accident report   Request to transfer to a special unit
Policy Manual   BOLO/APB

Application 2

Read the following description of a criminal act. Can you identify the audience?

Rewrite the case with a larger audience in mind. Remember to KISS it.

This case presents the ordinary man-that problem child of the law-in a most bizarre setting. As a lowly chauffeur in defendant's employ he became in a trice the protagonist in a breach-bating drama with a denouement almost tragic. It appears that a man, whose identity it would be indelicate to divulge, was feloniously relieved of his portable goods by two nondescript highwaymen in an alley near 26th Street and Third Avenue,

Manhattan; they induced him to relinquish his possessions by a strong argument ad hominem couched in the convincing cant of the criminal and pressed at the point of a most persuasive pistol. Laden with their loot, but not thereby impeded, they took an abrupt departure and he, shuffling off the coil of that discretion which enmeshed him in the alley, quickly gave chase through 26th Street toward 2d Avenue, whither they were resorting 'with expedition swift as thought' for most obvious reasons. Somewhere on that thoroughfare of escape they indulged the stratagem of separation ostensibly to disconcert their pursuer and allay the ardor of his pursuit. He then centered on for capture the man with the pistol whom he saw board defendant's taxicab, which quickly veered south toward 25th Street on 2d Avenue where he saw the chauffeur jump out while the cab, still in motion, continued toward 24th Street; after the chauffeur relieved himself of the cumbersome burden of his fare, the latter also is said to have similarly departed from the cab before it reached 24th Street. The chauffeur's story is substantially the same except that he states that his uninvited guest boarded the cab at 25th Street while it was at a standstill waiting for a less colorful fare; that his 'passenger' immediately advised him 'to stand not upon the order of his going but to go at once' and added finality to his command by an appropriate gesture with a pistol addressed to his sacro iliac. The chauffeur in reluctant acquiescence proceeded about fifteen feet, when his hair, like unto the quills of the fretful porcupine, was made to stand on end by the hue and cry of the man despoiled accompanied by a clamourous concourse of the law-abiding which paced him as he ran; the concatenation of 'stop thief,' to which the patter of persistent feet did maddingly beat time, rang in his ears as the pursuing posse all the while gained on the receding cab with its quarry therein contained. The hold-up man sensing his insecurity suggested to the chauffeur that in the event there was the slightest lapse in obedience to his curt command that he, the chauffeur, would suffer the loss of his brains, a prospect as horrible to an humble chauffeur as it undoubtedly would be to one of the intelligentsia. The chauffeur apprehensive of certain dissolution from either Scylla, the pursuers, or Charybdis, the pursued, quickly threw his car out of first speed in which he was proceeding, pulled on the emergency, jammed on his brakes and, although he thinks the motor was still running, swung open the door to his left and jumped out of his car. He confesses that the only act that smacked of intelligence was that by which he jammed the brakes in order to throw off balance the hold-up man who was half-standing and half-sitting with his pistol menacingly poised. Thus abandoning his car and passenger the chauffeur sped toward 26th Street and then turned to look; he saw the cab proceeding south toward 24th Street where it mounted the sidewalk. [A] mother and her two infant children were there injured by the cab which, at the time, appeared to be also minus its passenger who, it appears, was apprehended in the cellar of a local hospital where he was pointed out to a police officer by a remnant of the posse, hereinbefore mentioned. . . . Fortunately the injuries sustained were comparatively slight. (Cordas v. Peerless Transportation Co., 27 NYS2d 198)

Chapter 3

I Have to Write What?

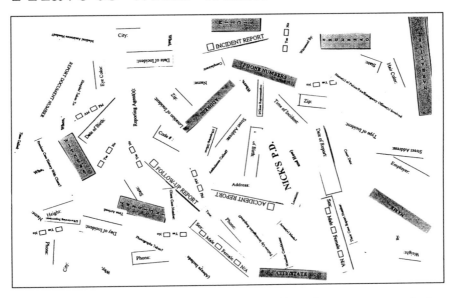

You've got all the pieces. That is, you've collected your notes—administrative or field—and identified your audience, so it's time to start generating your report. As we said in the last chapter, there are lots of ways to take field notes. Likewise, there are lots of ways to lay out a report on a page (the format). Our goal is not to force you into any one report format. Formats differ too much from agency to agency. Despite these differences, police reports, like other technical documents, share similar features. These features include technical vocabulary, visual cues, graphic aids, and objectivity. In addition, we use a high concentration of writing techniques such as description, process analysis, persuasion, and of course, narration. When used properly, these features enable you to write an effective report which can be interpreted only one way: a report which is accurate, accessible, clear, concise, complete, and objective.

NICK'S P.D.

☐ INCIDENT REPORT   ☐ ACCIDENT REPORT   ☐ FOLLOW-UP REPORT

REPORT DOCUMENT NUMBER

Date of Report:	Date of Incident:		Day of Incident:	Medical Assistance Needed? ☐ Yes ☐ No
				Ambulance Called? ☐ Yes ☐ No
Time of Incident:	Type of Incident:		Code # :	Time Called: _____ ☐ AM ☐ PM
				Time Arrived: _____ ☐ AM ☐ PM
Location of Incident:		Reporting Agent(s):		Hospital Taken To: _____
Name:	Sex: ☐ Male ☐ Female ☐ N/A		Date of Birth:	Photographs Taken? ☐ Yes ☐ No
Street Address:				By: _____
City:	State:	Zip:	Phone:	Witnessed By: _____
Employer:	Address:		Phone:	Follow-Up Investigation Required? ☐ Yes ☐ No
Name:	Sex: ☐ Male ☐ Female ☐ N/A		Date of Birth:	Arrest(s) Made? ☐ Yes ☐ No Complaint: _____
Street Address:				Court Date: _____
City:	State:	Zip:	Phone:	Location: _____
Height:	Weight:	Hair Color:	Eye Color:	Time: _____

NAME	ADDRESS	CITY/STATE	PHONE NUMBERS	Name(s) of Police/Fire/Emergency Officer(s) Involved
#1			(hm) (wk)	_____
#2			(hm) (wk)	Their Case Report Number: _____
#3			(hm) (wk)	Weather Conditions: _____

(Always Include Who, What, When, Where, Why, and How)

Previous Case History With Client? ☐ Yes ☐ No
Client Case Number: _____

_____ (narrative lines)

S/Reporting Officer: S/Reviewing Supervisor: S/Client Representative:

All good police reports must be accurate. You must take extreme care to make sure that you convey information with precision. On your radio, you use the phonetic alphabet to make sure that your audience (the dispatcher) knows exactly which letter(s) you are pronouncing. Similarly, in your reports you must make sure that all audiences will interpret your information in the same way. On one hand, this may be as simple as using Ø instead of a 0 in a VIN or using 7 instead of a 7. On the other hand, it may be as complex as reviewing your field notes and the report to make sure that all pertinent facts have been included. Inaccurate reports can cause you a great many problems as the following focus box illustrates.

From Internal Affairs*

All reports need to be complete and accurate. Officers die slow and agonizing deaths on a witness stand far more often than,

---

* Lt. C. Lee Bennett is currently head of Internal Affairs at the Springfield (MA) Police Department.

thankfully, from some criminal's gun or knife in 'real' life on the streets. They risk dire consequences when cutting reports short in a number of ways.

Most older officers I've ridden with and even some in the academy would, when pressed for "what it's really like out there," give the age-old advice to, "Make your reports brief. Don't give the defense attorneys or the brass too much to work with; after all, you'll remember the important stuff years later—a good cop always does."

Bull.

Nothing is more nerve racking than having to sit in a courtroom full of attorneys and your peers and be blasted out of the water because what was really important was not in your report. After forty-five minutes on the stand you can't remember your middle name, never mind what really happened six months ago when you made the arrest.

The fill-in-the-blank portions of the cover sheets of your incident reports are no less important. Accuracy is so important that one department furnishing us with sample reports used three different cover sheets during a six-month period. This department was looking for a cover sheet that had just the right combination of ease of use, versatility, and accuracy. Remember, though, that the best designed form is only as good as the person filling it out: garbage in, garbage out.

From the Report Review Unit*

The importance of getting the right name in the right box can best be illustrated by an example, unfortunately sad but true. The officer was sent to investigate a DOA (deceased person) which was apparently natural. The victim was an elderly male with a history of heart and respiratory problems. The next door neighbor provided the officer with relevant information. The officer then proceeded to record the name of the reporting person

* Lt. Helen Cooper is retired from the Chattanooga (TN) Police Department. She is currently with the Tennessee Criminal Justice Information Agency.

as the name of the victim, and the victim information as reporting person. The neighbor was reported as deceased for three days before he was resurrected by correcting the report.

All good police reports must be accessible. Your readers must be able to find (access) what they need. Most technical reports are processed by the receiver in either a linear or non-linear fashion; subsequently, you, as the encoder of a document, must ascertain the appropriate organization of your message and select the appropriate medium to facilitate processing by the decoder. OOPS! We just violated one of the most important rules of police writing; we forgot to KISS it. When all the fancy fluff is cut, what we really mean is that some people read reports straight through from the beginning to the end while others read them piecemeal, depending on what information they need. Let's go back to the example of the VCR for a minute. Some of us are linear readers. We sit down and read the entire manual as soon as we open the box. Most of us, though, especially those who have owned a VCR before, are non-linear readers. We scan the table of contents, look for the features that differ from our previous VCRs, and read only those sections that we need to know in order to operate the VCR.

Police reports are also read both ways. On one hand, an assistant prosecutor we know has developed a checklist for domestic violence reports. She will read each report linearly to determine whether or not all of the elements on her checklist are present. On the other hand, an insurance company's employee may scan a report, looking for only the information necessary to process a claim. Sometimes, a non-linear reader should be a linear reader. You can't rely on non-linear readers to catch your screwups. For example, how often does a supervisor approve a report by simply scanning the boxes?

From the in-service instructor*

The cover sheet of the report had all the information for a criminal mischief report, but the narrative had only the following:

---

* Michael Deppe is a retired police officer from the Lake Station (IN) Police Department. He instructs Report Writing at the Indiana Law Enforcement Training Academy and is a member of the Board of Directors of the Professionals Against Confidence Crime.

I Have to Write What? 27

Spam
Potatoes
Paper towels
Eggs
Bread
Milk 2%
Try to get movie for tonight

The officer later said he had intended to rewrite the report and was using it for a grocery list. The other interesting point was that the report was approved by the sergeant and passed through the lieutenant and on to the detective bureau.

Were the supervisors who approved this report linear readers?

How do you make your report accessible to both types of readers? You use headings and lists as visual cues. Think of these cues as street signs. Your readers can take the scenic route, driving down each of the main streets in your report, or they can quickly cruise through, looking for the avenue they need to travel. As we said earlier, formats differ. For example, one department may organize reports around the following descriptive headers:

- Information
- Initial Dispatch Information
- Venue
- Date and Time
- Victim
- Interview with Victim
- Suspect
- Interview with Suspect
- Witnesses
- Interview with Witnesses
- Arrests/Warrant Authorization
- Follow-up investigation
- Status

Yet, another department might use the ASCOT format:

- Arrest
- Source
- Circumstance of Incident
- Observations by Officers
- Taken (evidence, property, impound)

The headings may be radically different and there may be an argument over which format is best, but the information inside the report is still the same. Both meet the same goal. They are accessible. Whether you are writing a field report or an internal memo, these visual cues are essential for accessibility, allowing your reader to quickly find answers to the who, what, when, where, why, and how of your report.

While your report may be organized to improve access for your reader, it won't be any good if it is not clear. What was this officer trying to communicate in this **typewritten** report?

Writers given to P/R"s to 3407 on man shot from dispatch. Writers made 3407 main, to invest person shot. Writers t/t tenants that stated theirs no one shot here, but the guys ran to the vacant house on wildwood where they sell drugs. Writers made abv loc, that is when PO. Smith and PO. jones knock on the frt door while writer covered the rear of location. Writers then were led into the vacant dwelling by def #2. Writers ask #2 If he lived here, def stated no. Writers then heard from the basement stairs. While PO. Smith detained #2 writer and PO. Jones ran down to the basement, and obsv #4 at the bottom of stairs. Writer continued into basement and heard a metal rubbing sound coming from the northside of basement. Writer with my departmental issued flashlight illuminated the area next to the furnace, and obsv #1 using his left foot push qway the abv described weapons. Writer retrieved both hand guns, and ordered the def to get on his feet. Writer then obsv #3 hiding behind the furnace. Writer ordered #3 to his feet, and place both def"s that were in the basement into custody. PO. Jones detained #4. All def"s were conveyed to 3#dst for processing.

Good reports are always concise. It's important to understand, though, that concise does not mean short or brief. When a report is concise, it contains all the information necessary for your readers to understand exactly what occurred. Never sacrifice accessibility, accuracy, objectivity, clarity, or completeness on the altar of brevity. Be concise; don't worry about length. If you become preoccupied with length, you just might generate a report that is about as useful as the one discussed in the next focus box.

From the Report Review Unit

Many districts are plagued with repeat domestic violence callers who, until the Violence Against Women Act, were recorded simply as family disorders. I once picked up a group of domestic violence reports and, as I scanned them quickly, I noticed that the narrative of one report had the following: GTSOBOMHRN. I recognized the address as a regular and remembered hearing a family disorder call being dispatched earlier. When I inquired about the meaning, the officer said, "It's the same thing we hear every time. She says, 'Get that SOB out of my house right now.'" The officer rewrote the entire report.

On the other hand, you don't want to be too wordy and include too much irrelevant material because then your report could look something like this:

Random Thoughts from Sgt. Geoff

You got to write good reports because otherwise its just so much jibberjabber and nobody nos what the heck your getting at and its all over the place i mean first its one thing and then another an pretty soon you dont no yourself what you were trying to say and something you should have said at the beginning ends up at the end with no continuity or order and trying to read it is like trying to turn six nickels into a dollar and you give up and lose cases and crooks end up on the street and i dont no what all.

Good reports are complete. Your report is a record of your memory. It is a reconstruction of an event, backward in time, attempting to establish a sequence of activities as far as it can be determined. You become an historian, collecting all available information, organizing that information, and reporting all the facts regardless of whether or not you think it will hurt your case. If it isn't written down, it didn't happen. Complete reports can be your best friend; incomplete reports your worst enemy. Complete reports can be used as a tool to exonerate you; incomplete reports can be used as a tool to convict you.

From the Defense Attorney

The report itself must be as complete and accurate as possible. A common mistake police officers tend to make is to not include information in the report. There does not seem to be any single reason why information is omitted from the report. The typical explanation given by police officers when confronted by their omissions is, "I didn't think it was important." This explanation indicates that the officers are exercising discretion as to which matters will and will not be relevant to the attorneys trying the case. At worst, it appears that the officers are trying to withhold information from the defense. Even though that may not be the case, be assured that most defense counsel will attempt to make the jury believe that the officer's failure to include certain information was either intentional or negligent. In either situation, counsel will argue that neither the police nor their investigation can be relied on.

Good reports are always objective. You must always write so your report sounds as if it was written by an impartial third party. Reports must be written in an unbiased fashion and contain no attempt to arouse emotion. Most of the time, you will not have to be overly concerned about this due to the nature of the incident. However, some of your reports will deal with subjects which affect you emotionally. Writing reports about such cases will test your ability to remain objective. You do not have to use emotions to be persuasive. You can use objectivity to be **persuasive**. In fact, objectivity is a key element of persuasion. Remaining objective will lead to persuasion that is subtle and not at all overt. You are persuading the reader that your report is the work of a professional, that it is **objective**, complete, correct, and accurate. These features are your persuasive elements.

> **From the Prosecutor**
>
> Although writing such a report can be time consuming, it is crucial to a successful prosecution. Traditionally, assaultive crimes involving family members (domestic violence) are difficult to prosecute because the victims feel regret and guilt after calling 911. Preparing a detailed report, securing the victim's, witnesses', and suspect's statements at the scene, describing the demeanor of the individuals and the crime scene provides the Prosecutor the tools to effectively prosecute the case, with or without the victim. Victimless prosecution cannot succeed without the effort of the officers. *Treat these cases like homicide cases — prepare to win the case without the assistance of the victim.*

When we think about police reports, we tend to think only of reports done in the field following dispatched calls or observed incidents. You spend a great deal of time completing offense reports, incident reports, accident reports, supplemental reports, and closing reports. Don't forget, however, that your writing is not limited to those types of reports alone. (Remember Connect the Dots?) There are numerous other reports you use to communicate a thought, idea, or request. Use these same considerations when completing administrative reports in the form of a memo, complaint, query, or budget. Focus on accuracy, accessibility, clarity, conciseness, completeness, and objectivity.

Objectivity and the "I" word

If you don't use first person "I" in the narrative, your report may be accurate, complete, and objective, but it won't be clear, concise, or accessible. Typically, objective writing does not use the first person . For example, if you are a nonparticipant like a newspaper reporter, writing in the third person (not using I or you) is not a problem. Unfortunately, it becomes a problem when you are both a reporter of the facts (witness statements) and an active participant (arrests, bookings, seizures, etc.).

Police officers, in an attempt to appear objective, abandon writing in the first person. Worse yet, some officers become confused and switch back and forth between first and third person as the following quote illustrates.

> Writer with my departmental issued flashlight illuminated the area next to the furnace.

This attempt at objectivity sacrificed clarity. How many police officers does it take to hold a flashlight? Remember, being objective means being unbiased whether in a report or on the witness stand. Is the following sentence biased? Of course not.

> I used my departmental issued flashlight to illuminate the area next to the furnace.

Why would you make one statement in the written report and another on the witness stand? Third person writing has its uses, but not in most operational (field) reports. Formalized third person writing should be reserved for documents such as policies, procedures, rules, budgets, personnel orders, and proposals or papers presented at conferences.

Writing in the first person will overcome the confusion. Don't compound commotion with confusion. Stick to first person. KISS it.

As you observed in the samples used in the previous chapters, there are a lot of errors that can make your reports unusable. In the following chapters we will cover the most common, most easily made, most easily overlooked, and most easily fixed errors that can occur in your reports.

> **From the In-service Instructor**
>
> **A Generic Report Format.** In addition to the report formats discussed on pages 27–28, here is another format you may use in completing your narrative.

Introductory Information. I was dispatched to [where] at [what time] in regards to [what crime, incident, or offense]. Upon arriving at [what time], I met with [complainant, witness, or reporting party]. [Complainant, Witness, Reporting party name]stated that at [what time and date] he observed [who or what] at [where]. The offense occurred between [date and times].

Offense Details. I observed [entry, decedent, broken window, area where offense occurred]. It appeared as if [what]. The offense was committed by [how, i.e. hitting the victim].

Damage to People or Property. The [residence, vehicle, person] had [what] which appeared to be a result of [what or unknown means].

Victim and Witness Information. Name, date of birth, Social Security Number, address, home phone, work phone, work hours, and how to contact.

Your Actions. Complainant [directed to prosecutor, told to complete property list, etc.].

Actions by Other Officers. Officer [name] [secured scene for detectives or lab, notified owner, searched the building, filed supplemental report].

Suspect Information. Same as Witness plus height, weight, color of hair, color of eyes, scars, marks, tattoos, place of employment.

Victims Relationship to Suspect. [Victim, Witness, Complainant] has seen the suspect a few times at [where], works with the suspect [where], is related to the suspect [how], is a friend of the suspect [for how long?].

Springfield Police Department
Report Check List

Date of Incident_____   Time Frame_____

Victim Information #1   Sector _____

Name:_____
(Last)   (First)   (Middle)

Street Address:_____
(Number)   (Address)

Location of Incident:_____

City:_____ State:_____ Phone #:_____

S.S.#:_____ Lic/State:_____ DOB:_____

Suspect Information #1

Name:_____

Street Address:_____City:_____

SS#:_____Race:_____ DOB/Age:_____

Sex:____Weight:_____Height:_____Hair:_____Eyes:_____

Distinguishing Features:_____

Type of Weapon Used if Any_____

Suspect Information #2

Name:_____

Street Address:_____City:_____

SS#:_____Race:_____ DOB/Age:_____

Sex:____Weight:_____Height:_____Hair:_____Eyes:_____

Distinguishing Features:_____

Type of Weapon Used if Any_____

Offenses Committed

Type of Crime 1:_____2:_____

3:_____ Mode of Entry_____

Domestic: Y:☐ N:☐   Hate Crime: Y:☐ N:☐

Motor Vehicle Info:

M/V Reg #:_____ State:_____Yr:_____Make_____

Model:_____Type:_____Color:_____Vin#:_____

Use Reverse Side to write any Additional Info:

Exercises

1. Make a list of all the potential readers of your reports. Divide the list according to those who are linear readers and those who are non-linear readers.
2. Look at the sample report formats presented in this chapter. Identify which sections the non-linear readers will look at? (or, at which sections the non-linear reader will look?)*
3. *Scrambled Chunks.* The paragraphs below used to be a well written report. Using the structure provided, can you recreate the report?

Type of Report:
Initial Information:
Victim's Statement:
Officer's Actions:
Evidence:
Disposition:

---

1. #1-One Polaroid picture of the left side of MILTON's face.

---

2. At that point, MAY came to where MILTON was sitting on the Lazy-Boy in the living room, grabbed her by the hair and dragged her into the kitchen. MILTON is unsure which hand MAY used at which point. MAY threw MILTON on the floor of the kitchen, held her down with one hand, and hit her in the fare and head with the other. MAY used a closed fist, striking MILTON about the head six or seven times.

---

3. MILTON and MAY were not drinking or doing drugs but woke up about 0530 or 0600 hrs. on 25 January, 1998. Things were tense because they had decided to end their relationship. The argument this morning began when MAY could not find a piece of paper he wanted. MILTON told MAY she couldn't believe he was getting angry over a piece of paper.

---

* While it's not "technically" correct to end a sentence with a preposition, sometimes following some of the sillier rules of writing ruins clarity. As Winston Churchill was reported to have said, "Ending a sentence with a preposition is something up with which I shall not put."

4. Elizabeth Megan MILTON has been living with the accused, William Arthur MAY, for about two years. There have been several incidents of abuse where MILTON went to the hospital; she thought once to Southfield and twice to Central Medical, but she has not previously reported them.

5. Ofc.s PETTY and YINGLING assisted me by continuing to watch the house for a time, but saw no further movement from MAY. I provided MILTON with a CARE pamphlet, but since no arrest was made, I did not contact the agency.

6. Ofc.s PETTY and YINGLING were the first on scene, meeting MILTON at the Bay station. They saw the wound on MILTON's left cheek and took enough of a statement to discover that MAY hit MILTON. I joined the officers as they attempted to contact the accused, MAY.

7. Officers knocked on MAY's door for several minutes, even seeing him move around inside. MILTON advised that there was a dog inside and the dog would likely bite anyone who attempted to enter without MAY's permission. After moving to a safe location and taking MILTON's statement, I transported MILTON to a friend's house where she would stay until contacting her mother.

8. On 25 January 1998, I responded to 2108 E. Rooney to assist Ofc.s PETTY and YINGLING who were there on a domestic assault complaint. After taking a picture of her injuries, I took the victim's statement.

9. Report is Referred To Investigation.

10. MAY finally stopped and stood up, looking down over MILTON. MILTON got up and went out the backdoor. MAY grabbed a laundry basket of MILTON's belongings and set it outside the door. MILTON picked up the basket and went to the BAY gas station at Mohawk and Rooney to call us. MAY has a history of threatening people according to MILTON. MILTON does want to prosecute.

11. SIMPLE DOMESTIC ASSAULT

12. Since MILTON had a visible wound, I contacted Sgt. CARR, who brought over a Polaroid. I took one picture of the wound, showing the cut and abrasion on the left cheek bone of MILTON. I then tagged this into evidence.

Chapter 4

Who Did What to Whom?

In the beginning, the department created forms, and the Chief said this was good. And inscribed on stone the Chief first commanded "Thou shalt use the forms." And the Chief saw that it was good. And the officers toiled in the fields and used the forms. And the Chief saw that it was bad, and he wrote the second commandment "Thou shalt use the correct form." And the officers toiled in the fields and used the correct forms. And the Chief saw that it was bad, and he inscribed on the stone tablet, "Who Did What To Whom?"

This is why reports have two parts: (1) blanks or boxes, and (2) empty pages. Once you figure out what you're writing about and why you're writing—your purpose and audience—you need to go to the shelf where the forms are kept and pick the right one. Now what? You fill in the form. Usually the blanks and boxes are pretty easy as long as you get the right information in the right box. Remember the witness who was the dead person and the dead person who was the witness? Then, you are confronted with a blank page (often called a continuation) that may or may not contain pre-printed lines. This blank page can be tough to fill, especially if your cage has recently been rattled.

From the Trainer

At 6 a.m., my partner and I responded to a suspicious persons call. I was tired, and I relaxed too soon. The next thing I remember was a gun pointed at my stomach. Fortunately, I managed to disarm the subject. It was the closest I had ever come to laying my mortgage on the doorsteps of the finance company. We took the subject, a convicted armed robber wanted for a parole violation, into custody. When we got back to the station, I started to write the report. The fill-in-the-blanks were easy. The narrative was impossible.

This street cop admits to having trouble with his narrative, a term we first used in chapter three. But what is a narrative? A narrative is a time-ordered sequence of events. It is the simplest and most commonly used way of organizing communication. Whether we are aware of it or not, all of us have extensive experience with narratives; we've been using narratives since we first began to speak. The books we read, the movies or television programs we watch, the stories we tell to friends: all are narratives. We begin at the beginning and relate every relevant event that occurred until the end. In other words, begin with what initiated your action, relate the action(s) taken, and conclude with the results. Got it? Do we need to say more? Well, yes. Structuring the police narrative usually is not quite that simple.

Most of the time, your report is not based on what you actually saw. Someone else either witnessed or was involved in the incident and called the police. Dispatch initiated your involvement. To complicate matters even further, much (if not all) of the event has played itself out by the time that you arrive on the scene. If all of the world is a stage, your role may not begin until Act II, Scene 1. In fact, all too often your role doesn't begin until the play is over. And since you missed the play entirely, you must interview the audience to find out exactly what happened on the stage. This makes structuring your narrative a bit difficult.

Since a narrative is a time-ordered sequence of events, the reporting officer must make the time frame clear. The reporting officer must begin that officer's narrative with that officer's involvement. The reporting officer either receives the call from dispatch or a citizen flags the reporting officer down. The reporting officer then relates the events as they occur. WHOA! What is wrong with these sentences? As we wrote in the last chapter, abandon the rigid, artificial third person in favor of a more readable first person in your narrative. Let's try it this way. The narrative is time ordered, so you must make the time frame clear. Begin your narrative with your involvement. You either received a call from dispatch, observed an incident yourself, or a citizen flagged you down. You then relate the events as they occur, using headings and subheadings to help your reader understand the time frames involved. For example, you may begin to structure your narrative with the following headings: Initial Dispatch Information; Venue; Date and Time. After these segments have been filled in, they would look something like:

- Initial Dispatch: At 3:00 a.m. on 07-01-99, I was dispatched to a suspicious activity complaint at Apartment 3C, 2801 Lane Drive.
- Venue: This incident occurred at Apartment 3F, 2801 Lane Drive, located in Leonidas township, St. Joseph county, state of Michigan.
- Date and Time: This incident occurred on 07-01-99 at 12:40 a.m.

Your involvement then starts in the next section which might begin with the heading *Observations*. This is where you record the facts of the incident as you witnessed them. As you do this, remember that facts are observable actions or real, physical things; everything else is opinion. The statement, "The suspect was acting strangely" is an opinion. The statement "The suspect, who was sitting naked in the middle of the intersection, stated that he was waiting for aliens from Omicron 7 to beam him up," is a fact.

Within the *Observations* segment of the narrative, use subheadings to let your reader know what type of facts you are recording. Some of the facts you will collect personally, such as the identification of people with whom you speak, descriptions of the scene, what evidence you seized, and so forth. Some of the facts you get secondhand, such as those given you by a witness. Witness statements are identified as such and recorded exactly as given. Subheadings in your narrative may look something like:

Suspect #1: Name, race and gender, birth date, address, telephone #.
Interview with Witness #1: Name, race and gender, birth date, address, and telephone #, followed by his/her statement.

These headings and subheadings serve two functions: they act as cues for your readers, and they help organize your narrative.

Knowing how to structure and organize a narrative is great. You may have filled in all of the boxes correctly and used headings and subheadings to organize your narrative, but if your sentences do not make sense, the Chief will probably smack you with the stone upon which his commandments were engraved because he still does not know "*Who Did What To Whom.*"

Your narrative is a record of *Who, Did What, To Whom*. Most, if not all of that information can be found in your field notes. But before you can put the narrative together, there are a few (and we are sorry we have to use such a dirty word) grammar concepts that must be considered. Grammar is the set of rules and procedures by which we generate sentences, that is communicate in writing. One of the basic rules of grammar is that all complete sentences must have at least one somebody or something (subject) doing something (verb); for example, I (who) shot (did what). The following sentence has both a subject and a verb. But is it right?

> Officers was dispatched to 123 Main Street.

Having a subject and verb doesn't make your sentence right. You will look anything but professional if your subject and verb don't agree (remember "If you write like a idiot, they think you a idiot"?). That is, if you use a plural subject, you must use a plural verb. Say what? Again, a fancy term for a simple concept. The above example can be fixed quite easily. In fact, this example illustrates one of the most common errors of this type. Just remember if it happened *now*...

Who	Did What
I	Am
He/she/it	Is
We/you/they	Are

If it happened in the *past*...

Who	Did What
I	Was
He/she/it	Was
We/you/they	Were

Apply this and you get

> Officers were dispatched to 123 Main Street.

But you don't always use am/is/was/were, so it isn't always this easy to fix. For example, we wouldn't write the sentence:

> The officer drive the car.

Instead, we would write:

> The officer drives the car.

But what if we have more than one officer? Would it be:

> The officers drives the car.

No, of course not. Subjects and verbs like these must agree in number:

> The officers drive the car.

Use your powers of observation and perception. See a pattern here? Notice how if you move your "s" the correction is made? Another simple rule: look at the noun and verb; there can only be one "s." Note to those grammarians out there: it is possible to find exceptions to this rule, but none that are important to our reports.

Who	Did What (Now/Present)
Officer Officers	Arrests Arrest
Suspect Suspects	Resists Resist
Victim Victims	Moans Moan

Fortunately (or not) this type of error most often occurs in internal reports and memoranda because field reports are always written in the past tense.

Who	Did What (Then/Past)
Officer Officers	Arrested
Suspect Suspects	Resisted
Victim Victims	Moaned

It is when you forget that field reports are written in the past tense that you can get yourself in trouble. Sometimes, your mind even wanders in mid-sentence and you end up shifting tenses:

> Complainant states she called her sister for a ride home, and then report later to Station 2.

How would your correct this sentence?

There are some errors with verb tense that cops do make, though. These are most often related to the irregular verbs. And no, these are not verbs that need Metamucil. The irregular verbs are those that don't simply add an -ed to the end to make them past tense; the whole word will change. For example:

> He shoot the house.
> He just get off of parole.

If you add an -ed to fix these sentences, they will look like this:

> He shooted the house.
> He just geted off of parole.

There are just some action words you will have to remember: shoot/shot, get/got, run/ran and so forth.

> He shot the house.
> He just got off of parole.

At the end of this chapter, we've supplied you with a list of these words. Keep it in your clip board and refer to it as necessary.

Some actions, though, require someone or something to receive them; the recipient of the action is the "*To Whom*" (object). The example "I shot," has a noun and a verb, but what or who received the action? This is where the "*To Whom*" becomes important. The object is the third and final critical element in the typical sentence. Now we have *Who Did What To Whom*. I shot the dog.

"The suspect was observed breaking the window."

Sounds like a good sentence doesn't it? But, let's apply the commandment "*Who Did What To Whom?*" Well, the suspect broke the window. But there is another action here: was observed. There is something missing. *Who* did the observing of whom? Look at the sentence again. We can see that the suspect was observed, but there is no one doing the observing. There must always be someone or something performing any action you record.

Sentences without someone or something performing the action frequently are found in administrative reports, internal memos, and poorly written field reports. Start looking at the administrative reports and internal memos you receive. For example,

"Feedback has indicated that there is a deficiency of report writing skill in this department."

or

"It has been determined that military drill will increase the cohesion of recruits during training."

Have you ever received a memo that sounded like these? Apply "*Who Did What To Whom?*" Where did the feedback come from? *Who* collected it? *Who* determined that military drill would be helpful? How was this determination made? If sentences sound like this, it is usually because the writer does not want to go out on a limb, lacks the nerve to take responsibility for the decision or action, or did not read this book. As you can see, failure to carefully follow the Chief's commandment results in confusion and more questions being asked than are being answered. Don't do this to your audience. Try applying the commandment to this report.

From the files

When the property was brought back to the station, it was discovered that it was the stolen property.

Break this down and place the important information into the columns below.

Who?	Did What?	To Whom?
?	brought back	the property
?	discovered	?
?	was	?

Raises a lot of questions, doesn't it? Let's fix it.

I brought the hand gun back to the station. I ran a computer check of the serial number. I got an NCIC hit.

Who?	Did What?	To Whom?
I	brought	the hand gun
I	ran	a computer search
I	got	an NCIC hit

The repaired version is clearer, but it reads like Tarzan said it. While we will get into other parts of the sentence in later chapters, keep in mind that if you only use the *Who Did What To Whom* narrative structure, your reports will indeed sound like a "Tarzan" movie or a first grade reader: Look, look. See Spot. See Spot run. Run Spot, run. It's obvious that you need more than *Who Did What To Whom* to get the information across clearly. But as you begin to increase the complexity of your sentences, you also increase the chances that you will make some basic errors like "The victim was shot in the kitchen." Which leads us to the next chapter.

Exercise in Organization

The sentences below used to be a well written and structured narrative. Using the structure provided, can you recreate the report?

Type of Report:
Information:
Venue:
Date and Time:
Complainant Information:
Interview with Complainant/Witness Enrico Caruso:
Suspect and Suspect Vehicle:
Stolen Property:
Case Status:

1. CARUSO told me that two or three white males came into the store and were talking to him briefly, asking him where he was from.

2. He believes he would recognize the car if it returned to the station and possibly the suspects, although his description was very minimal.

3. He described the car as a large, 4-door, brown car.

4. He said the car, being only described as a large brown 4-door, left eastbound on Gull and then took a left turn onto Grunwald, where he lost sight of it.

5. He turned to look outside and noticed one white male jump from the rear of a large brown 4-door vehicle and grab two, 2 liter bottles of pop from the display case right in front of the store, hop back into the car and then leave the area.

6. He was also not sure of the brand of car, as he is not very familiar with American cars.

7. His acquaintances were also described as white males in their early 20's.

8.   On the below date and time, an unknown subject stole two bottles of pop from in front of the TEXACO GAS STATION at 1070 Red Bird Drive.

9.   Stolen were two, 2 liter bottles of Coke, valued at $2.00 total.

10. The case can be considered inactive at this time pending any further investigative leads.

11. The clerk on duty was ENRICO CARUSO, a white male, DOB 03-21-78, home address of 1170 Ibis, #213, Casselberry, Florida, 32707, phone 339-6397.

12. The clerk was able to give no physical description, such as clothing or facial features.

13. The clerk was not able to describe the suspect or the other two acquaintances very well. He only described them as white males in their early 20's.

14. The clerk was provided a copy of the case number for store records.

15. The complainant is the TEXACO GAS STATION at 1070 Red Bird Drive.

16. The incident occurred at 1070 Red Bird Drive, in the township and county of Casselberry, state of Florida.

17. The incident occurred on 07-20-97 at 2:04 a.m.

18. The suspect was only described as a white male in his early 20's.

19. Theft.

20. They bought some items from inside the store and exited shortly thereafter.

Did What Words That Don't Use -ed

bend	bent	hold	held	sink	sank
bind	bound	keep	kept	sit	sat
bite	bit	kneel	knelt	sleep	slept
bleed	bled	know	knew	slide	slid
break	broke	lay	laid	speak	spoke
bring	brought	(to put)		speed	sped
buy	bought	lead	led	spend	spent
catch	caught	lie (to	lay	spin	spun
come	came	recline)		spit	spat
deal	dealt	lose	lost	stand	stood
dig	dug	make	made	steal	stole
dive	dove	mean	meant	stick	stuck
do	did	meet	met	sting	strung
draw	drew	mistake	mistook	stink	stunk
drink	drank	pay	paid	strike	struck
drive	drove	plead	pled	swear	swore
eat	ate	prove	proved	swim	swam
fall	fell	ride	rode	swing	swung
feel	felt	ring	rang	take	took
fight	fought	run	ran	teach	taught
find	found	say	said	tear	tore
flee	fled	see	saw	tell	told
freeze	froze	seek	sought	think	thought
get	got	sell	sold	throw	threw
give	gave	send	sent	wake	woke
go	went	shake	shook	wear	wore
have	had	shine	shone	win	won
hear	heard	shoot	shot	wind	wound
hide	hid	show	showed	write	wrote

Exercises

Revise the following sentences, making sure that the *Who* and *Did What* agree in number.

1. Writers responded to above loc. & was met by P.R.O. who stated that she observed (1) B/M break out a car window in the alley across from above loc.
2. Officers was dispatched to 711 West Middle Street.
3. Upon arrival at the scene both Megan Schwartz and her live-in boyfriend, Billy Joe Bach, was sitting in a blue Pontiac Grand Am or similar vehicle.
4. The purse, planner, and money was released to compl.
5. I then asked Lolita for permission to search her coat, backpack, and purse/wallet that was on the floor next to her.
6. Both escapees was positively ID at the scene.
7. He and the driver Lloyd Miller both was order to the ground at gunpoint.
8. Complainant admitted to hospital security that she took money which were to be deposited into the hospital's account to pay for her son's drug habit.
9. The suspects was arrested for discharging a firearm into an occupied dwelling and CCW auto.
10. Officers was working a two men unit.

Did you notice that five of these sentences were missing something? Remember "It has been determined that..."? Rewrite the five sentences. Add what you think is necessary to answer your readers' questions.

Correct the errors with the *Did What* words in the following sentences. Keep in mind that your narrative is typically written after the event has occurred.

1. Wrt. enter loc. w/Unt 2123 Wrtrs. find abv. subj. S/E slide of business.
2. Writer yelled for subject to stop vehicle, at which time subject looked in writer's direction, and then back over active fire hose from Engine 22 again.
3. Complainant states abovev Perp send a letter to Complainant's home.
4. Perp park F/O abv location blowing the horn of perp's veh.

5. Smith threatened Jones by saying he will shot the house up.
6. At approximately time /loc. abv. compl. states he was carjack at abv. loc.
7. Writer use fire extingusher to put out fire.
8. The front passenger window busted out and steering wheel + dash board area damage.
9. The compl. show visible injuries to officer.
10. I yell to Judge Marlow to hit the alarm.

Chapter 5

What Part of the Anatomy
Is the Kitchen?

> Upon arriving at the scene, I realized that the victim had been
> shot in the kitchen.

What part of the anatomy is the kitchen? It really sounds painful. Did
the officer who wrote this narrative really mean what was written? This
sentence was part of a well-structured narrative, and it seems to be a well-
formed sentence. It appears then, that knowing how to structure a narrative and what makes up a sentence is not enough. You are not ready to
get on with report writing. There are a few more things to learn about the
basic sentence. You've answered the questions about *Who, Did What,*
and *To Whom* in your sentences. But this is still not enough. It's more
than just each sentence having someone doing something to someone. To
let your readers know exactly what occurred, use specific details. You can
do this by having a series of short sentences each containing an additional detail. But as you saw in the previous chapter, such a report will sound
like a first grade reading text or a Tarzan movie script. You will end up
with a narrative that sounds something like "I saw the vehicle. The vehicle was the suspect's. The vehicle was red. The vehicle had four doors.
The vehicle was a Yugo. The vehicle was heading west." Get the picture?
If not, consider a career where you'll ask, "Do you want fries with that?"
How can you add the necessary detail without sounding like Tarzan?

Add detail using single words or clusters of words. It is not difficult,
but like anything else in writing, there are several places where you can
get into a bit of trouble. What a surprise, huh? How do you add the
details without confusing your reader? Use the *Who,* the *Did What,* or
the *To Whom* as an anchor for your detail. Think of the *Who/Did
What/To Whom* as center mass of the silhouette target on the firearms

53

range. The detail words are the bullets. You have to keep the bullets in the center of mass. In other words, you have to keep your detail words near the thing or action they are describing (center mass words). What you end up with is a sentence containing the necessary specific detail. "I saw the suspect's red, four-door Yugo heading west on Main Street." Reads a bit better, doesn't it? Other benefits are that your report will take less time to write, be more concise, and be easier to read.

There are two kinds of detail that can be added to any sentence. First, you can add detail to the "who" words. Keep in mind that we are using the word "who" very liberally. As we first introduced in Chapter 4, *Who*, in addition to a person, can also be a place or a thing like an intersection, city, gun, and so forth. The words that add detail to the *Who* are everyday words like make, model, sex, age, race, height, weight, etc. For example, you can have a blue, F-150, short-box pick up truck, or you can have a 6'4", 250#, white male, approximately 48 years old. If you strip out the detail, you are back in the jungle with Tarzan and are left with a truck or a male. Second, you can add detail to the *"Did What"* words. "The postal employee *repeatedly* shot the supervisor," or "The suspect *loudly* demanded money from the teller." As Dr. Suess would say, let's begin by taking a look at all the Whos in Whoville.

Perhaps you've noticed that each time we add detail we keep that detail and the word it describes close to each other. A good rule of thumb is that if the descriptive word is more than one or two words away, you could be making a serious mistake (think center mass). For example,

> "...made a traffic stop of 86 Chev 2dr Red Mi plt# ZFR386 for speeding."

If you were to check your *Identification and Information Manual*, you would find that Michigan plates are not red. Wait a minute, though. The detail is only two words away at the most. So let's apply another rule of thumb. When we use single words to add detail, we usually place them to the left of the word they are describing. It may help to keep in mind that we seldom pass on the right, and we seldom put single detail words on the right. If your detail word is to the right of what it is describing, it has the potential to be misunderstood. So rearrange the detail.

"...made a traffic stop of a red, 86 Chev., 2dr, MI tag ZFR386 for speeding." (Remember CYMBOL*?)

How about this one?

"...driven by a white male in his 20's with blond hair approximately 5'10" tall."

Rearranged, it reads:

"...driven by a white male in his 20's, approximately 5'10" tall, with blond hair."

---

*Color, Year, Make, Body, Occupants/Other, License

Did you notice that in the second example some of the detail, like "white," is on the left while some, like "in his 20's," is not? There is a reason for this. Sometimes, we use clusters of words to add detail. Unlike single words, these clusters can go on either side of the word being described. But guess what? Just like single words, be careful where you use them. There are two very effective ways to avoid getting into trouble with detail words and clusters.

First, you can follow the report format in your department's report writing manual or NCIC manual. If you do, you will notice that descriptions of the "*Who*" are usually arranged in a logical order: name, race, sex, DOB, height, weight, hair color, eye color. A second way? Think center mass. Keep the detail word or phrase and the word it adds detail to CLOSE TOGETHER. Applying either of these methods you end up with a:

> "...white male in his 20's, approximately 5'10" tall, with blond hair."

Misplaced clusters can be found anywhere in a sentence—at the beginning, middle, or end. Regardless of where the cluster is placed, it can make for some unusual situations (and some fun reading). Can you identify the misplaced clusters in the following reports?

> "...when I came upon a vehicle parked in the southeast corner of the lot with three white males in it."

Three Men and a Parking Lot. Wasn't that a Tom Selleck movie?

> "She stated the money was put in its usual place below the floor under the top part of the safe, unlocked."

Was the floor, the money, or the safe unlocked? See what happens when you don't keep the clusters close to what they describe?

Some clusters can only be used to add detail to a *Who*. It is not as hard as it sounds. These clusters are easy to spot because they only start with one of seven words: that, which, who, whose, whoever, whom, and whomever. Anytime a cluster begins with one of these words, the cluster must be placed immediately to the right of the word it describes.

Also, remember a *Who* can be a person, place, or thing. A person is not a *that*. A person is not a *which*. A person is a *Who*. A person can also be a *whose*, a *whoever*, a *whom*, or a *whomever*. When you add a detail cluster to a person, begin the cluster with a *Who* word. When you add a detail cluster to a *Who* that is a place or thing, use *that* or *which*. Take a look at this sentence from a vehicle burglary report.

> "He also had stereo components in the rear of the Suburban that was not touched."

Very interesting. We have a suspect who is capable of removing items from the Suburban without touching the vehicle. The detail cluster starts with the right word, but we hope it is just in the wrong place. By the way, did you catch the other error? Or, how about this one:

> "...attempt to locate a student on campus that may be using the vehicle."

We wonder if the campus has a driver's license? The cluster is adding detail to a person, so it should start with a *Who*. The cluster also needs to be moved so that it is near the center mass of the target word, in this case student.

When this officer recovered a stolen bicycle, ask yourself what matched the victim's description. Remember, read exactly what is there. Don't assume.

"I found a red GT BMX under a bed inside the apartment that matched the description the victim had given."

Sometimes, just when you think that you have it all figured out, you don't. Can you spot any problems with this sentence?

"Running after the suspect, my weapon unintentionally discharged."

You've got a cluster to the left of the word it is describing. It doesn't start with one of the seven words. It must be OK. Think like a cop. There are crimes of commission and crimes of omission. We talked about the crimes of commission above (misplaced clusters). Which type of crime did this officer commit? Do you know? Reconstruct this incident in your mind. We did, so take a look.

"RUNNING AFTER THE SUSPECT, MY WEAPON UNINTENTIONALLY DISCHARGED."

This is a crime of omission. The problem here was not that the detail word was in the wrong place or that the word it was describing was in the wrong place. The problem was that the word being described was AWOL.* While you might have thought the word was there, i.e. my, it really wasn't. You had to assume what the writer really meant. When you read or write reports, you can't assume anything. False assumptions in police work are one of the *10 Fatal Errors*. Read what is on the page.

"Running after the suspect, my weapon unintentionally discharged."

Can you can fix it without adding another *Who*? No. It can't be done. What is the cluster "running after the suspect" adding detail to? My? No, because "my" is not a *Who* word, it is a detail word adding to the *Who* word "weapon." The first *Who* word in this sentence is weapon. Weapons can't run. Someone has to be running.

"I was running after the suspect when my weapon unintentionally discharged."

Or,

"While I was running after the suspect, my weapon unintentionally discharged."

If your reader has to fill in gaps created by words which are AWOL, you not only missed center mass, you threw the round completely off the target. Try it on these examples:

"Smiling proudly, the commendation was presented to the officer."

---

* Absent Without Leave

> "Sitting for a moment, the undercover officer's eyes looked around at the other people in the restaurant."

Just imagine: a smiling commendation or a pair of eyeballs that can sit on a table. Identify the AWOL *Who* words, put them in the sentences, and you will get

> "Smiling proudly, the chief presented the commendation to the officer."

> "While the undercover officer sat for a moment, he looked at the people in the restaurant."

Now that we have added detail to the *Who*, we will add detail to the *Did What*. *Did What* words are usually the action taking place. Use clusters to answer questions about When, Where, and How. These clusters can be found on either side of this action word, but should be kept near the center of mass.

What did this officer mean?

> "While at the location, Johnson Alarm Company called and writers answered the phone."

The officer is actually saying that the alarm company was at the location of the alarm and the writers (we can only assume the writers were officers) were at some unknown location. So, we rearrange the words to keep the detail close to either the *Did What* or the *Who*.

> "While at the location, we answered the phone when the Johnson Alarm Company's dispatcher called."

Not only was the detail cluster in the wrong place, there were also some other problems that needed to be fixed. Did you catch the problems? We had to change the narrative to first person (Chapter 3), and we had to find the AWOL *Who* because companies can't use telephones—they don't have fingers.

The detail clusters that answer the *When?* must be placed carefully, but they are easy to spot. They usually start with words like after, before, during, when, and while. The detail clusters that answer the *Where?* are also easy to spot. Just remember what a squirrel can do to a tree.

A squirrel can go: up, in, out, around, over, between, behind, down, through, under, among, at, to, toward, away, next, into, beside, onto, above, across, against, a tree.

Squirrels? Trees? Clusters? You probably think (know) we are nuts. But try it.

Through the window, I saw the suspect crawling.

Is the detail cluster easy to spot? Yes. It is *through the window.* But, move the detail cluster (accidentally or on purpose) and you get an entire different meaning.

I saw the suspect crawling through the window.

Try another one.

Writers given P/R's to 307 Main on a man shot from dispatch.

Visualize *exactly* what was written. We did.

"...MAN SHOT FROM DISPATCH."

You can also add detail to the *Did What* using single words. These words are very common and easy to spot. They only add detail to the *When* (how often) and the *How* (how much or what manner). They also usually end in *-ly*. When you use single detail words to add to the *Did What*, you can run into two problems. First, most of these detail words are subjective and do not belong in a police report. They reflect opinion and they lack precision. Which of the following frequency statements is more precise?

Stabbed multiple times.

Stabbed approximately 37 times.

He was acting strangely.
He was sitting naked in the intersection waiting for aliens from Omicron 7 to pick him up.

Second, those few that do work in a police report can be put in the wrong place and radically alter the meaning of the sentence. Can you find the misplaced detail word or cluster in the following sentences?

"...firing approximately two shots through front storm door striking #1 as she stood near door in right side of jaw."

"...Schmidt does his stalking in a vehicle in color with stripes."

The title of this chapter is a classic example of one of the errors of misplacing a detail phrase. How would you fix it?

Now that we've completed our sweep of the detail scene, we need to go back and make sure we've located all the pitfalls. Lurking in the dark corners are what we can only describe as those nasty little single words that can give you fits. Harmless little detail words like only, just, almost, even, exactly, and nearly. Shifting these words in the sentence is like putting your car in reverse at 50 MPH. It does a lot of damage. For example:

"I only fired one round."   "Only I fired one round."
"I just hit a pedestrian."   "I hit just a pedestrian."
"The instructor almost   "The instructor flunked
    flunked all of them."   almost all of them."

If you can get all of this chapter straight, congratulate yourself—you've done good. OOPS! There is one last thing you should remember. Good adds detail to a *Who*. Well adds detail to a *Did What*. So, now, if you can get all of this chapter straight, congratulate yourself. You've done well. Good job!

Exercises

The sentences below contain both crimes of commission and crimes of ommission. Move detail words or clusters and add *Who* words as necessary.

1. Writer inserted head through broken screen window & looked down, observing a purse laying down on street fitting description of compl's purse.
2. I observed the above location with the front window broken out upon our arrival.
3. Writer made scene compl outside pointed out subj at end of block who had left business without paying food bill #351-024 $37.21.
4. The above vehicle was impounded by Stephens Tow w/keys.
5. W/unk cal. handgun firing approx 2 shots through front storm dr. striking #1 as she stood near dr. in r/side of jaw.
6. With the commotion in the bedroom Rodney Markle stated that his friend John, who had invited him over, came into the bedroom and held onto his brother James to keep him from getting involved.
7. Cooper will flee to his mother's house who lives in Nunica.
8. As I neared the exit where the vehicle was approaching, I saw that it was a dark Chevy Blazer with tinted windows.
9. As reporting officer arrived, I could see that the left front tire was flat on Helen's car.
10. Mr. Walker told this officer on the inside of his residence that he had been the victim of a breaking and entering.
11. When asked to count or recite the alphabet it was evident that his speech was slurred in all instances.
12. Nudelman stated after waiting in the bushes for a bit, Berko began to come out of the apartment.
13. He indicated that the cup with his finger would be about 4 inches tall.

14. Officer Chaffee spoke with Despain and got a description of the direction where the suspect fled on foot and attempted a search with his canine.
15. Healy had a minor cut on his upper lip located underneath of his lip.
16. That a man had arrived at 422 6th Street armed with a handgun threatening suicide.
17. She advised her parents that she received the stolen tickets along with her girl friend Mary Bacon, from a boy named Richard Allen.
18. Writers then interviewed the passenger in the above vehicle & found her to be using an alias wanted on felony warrant.
19. Unit in full uniform and full marked squad car made a traffic stop of 96 chev 2dr red tx plt# ibm 386 for speeding.
20. Compl stated she was driving into the rear of her residence when she (compl) observed above subject standing at the rear of her residence in the driveway.
21. Wrt's partner Officer Verberg found abv. subject hiding in bathroom fitting same description according w/compl.
22. Suspect has thrown car keys that have hit her in a fit of temper.
23. The victim stated that the suspect loaded his semi-truck into his Volks Wagon auto.
24. 911 calls were received form both the interior of the store and the exterior pay phone of the store.
25. It should be noted that the identities of the three boys at the residence prior to this incident's occurrence being only identified in the narrative as Bill, Al, and Rick are not known.
26. The victim in this case Andrea Doria was sent to the Central Hospital emergency room in the custody of her mother.
27. Sipe advised me that shortly after 6:00 a.m. on 09-12-98, he was walking out to his car near 6767 W. Summit and observed a very young child wandering around the apartment complex, who appeared distraught and was looking for her mother.
28. One of the b/m struck victim in the living room.
29. The suspect was identified by his driver's license which was later arrested with an accomplice.
30. Both weapons was loaded and made safe by officers Rodney and Walusayi after the Crime Lab photographed them at the scene.

Chapter 6

What I Meant, Not What I Wrote

> # ASLET (not) LAX about Use of Force Training

—Police Sept. 97

"Words mean something." — Rush Limbaugh

Whether or not you agree with the politics Rush preaches, you have to admit that he was right on target when he said this. Words do, indeed, mean something. Reread the above headline. What was the author trying to convey? What was actually conveyed? Every word or symbol means something. In this case, the author wanted to stress that ASLET is not lax when it comes to training. The symbol makes the headline read ASLET is NOT not LAX about Use of Force Training. In other words, ASLET is lax about use of force training. It was not what the writer meant, but it was what he wrote.

THE THING COPS FIND MOST ANNOYING ABOUT ENGLISH-MAJOR GANGS

"Speed Bump." Copyright 1996 by Creator's Syndicate, Inc.
Used by permission of the artist.

Sometimes, you look at your report and you feel an urge to use a $64 word where a 5¢ word will work just as well. All of us whose jobs require writing fall prey to this urge. Perhaps we are tired of using the same words again and again and again, or maybe we're trying to impress our readers for whatever purpose. You may think that you must use the "big" words since your report will often end up in court and you want to use the proper "legalese." Actually, this is not necessary. You are not a lawyer writing for other lawyers. You are a law enforcement officer writing for a varied audience. Your purpose is to prepare reports that are clear and concise, not to draft legal documents.

"Speed Bump." Copyright 1998 by Creator's Syndicate, Inc.
Used by permission of the artist.

Be clear and concise; the lawyers and judges will appreciate it. They are quite capable of messing up what you have written all by themselves. As a matter of fact, the legal profession is moving away from the use of "legalese" and is adopting the use of plain English. Help them along. Use *Plain English for Cops*. If you are tempted to reach for a thesaurus, regardless of the reasons, STOP FOR A MINUTE AND THINK. Your primary endeavor is to convey a semantic meaning and to eschew obfuscation. OOPS. Your ultimate goal (as we've said time and time again) is to communicate clearly with your reader. In other words, KISS it.

Read the following sentence from a Felonious Assault/Malicious Destruction of Property report.

> In addition, the victim stated that he was cut with a small pen knife during the affray.

Is the term "affray" a common, nontechnical word that is generally understood by everyone, or does it have a unique meaning? In fact, do people with a higher education know what it means? What exactly did the officer mean? A quick check of the *American Heritage Dictionary* tells us that an affray is a noisy quarrel or brawl and urges us to look up "conflict" to find words with similar meanings. Flipping to conflict, we find that affray suggests a public fight or brawl. So far, so good. But when we look at the sample sentence showing us how to use affray, we find "Yet still the poachers came for affrays in woods and on moors with liveried armies of keepers." Huh? Does affray describe what really happened? Sure it does. Five kids took a bicycle from another child at knifepoint. The victim was cut while he was trying to keep ahold of the bike. So the officer did use this word correctly, but he violated one of the main rules of word usage — use the common word, not the uncommon one. Do you think others in your chain of command or report review unit will appreciate having to turn to a dictionary to find out what happened? Save the big, off-the-wall words for SCRABBLE™. You need to appreciate how you might sound to the reader. Strive to sound like a law enforcement professional, not a pompous, stuffy professor. For example,

> I did inquire from Meier why she waited so long to report the incident.

Did the officer mean "I asked"? What did the officer mean in the following?

> I spoke with Kristin Meier at Parkway Hospital's E.R. and the following information was disclosed.

Does this mean "she told me"?

Sometimes, in an attempt to write like the two officers above, you end up with something like the following:

> After an extensive over 15 minute observation period[the suspect] did not belch, vomit, or regurgitate.

Extensive is a nice word and relatively common. But its dictionary definition suggests that a possible meaning is "extended." Would anybody, other than a four-year-old sitting in a time-out chair, consider fifteen minutes an extended period of time? It really wasn't necessary for the officer to add a descriptive word to this sentence. It would be simpler and more professional to say, "During a 15 minute observation period...."

Even when you try to use the more common word, you may leave your report open to several interpretations. For example,

> His speech was slightly slurred and he continued to have a numb look to his face.

This officer used the detail word numb, which is hardly a "pompous" word. But what exactly is a numb look? Did the subject stare ahead without recognizing anyone? Was his face sagging like a lip after a visit to the dentist? Had he suffered a stroke? Look at the next example. The officer left her reader with at least three unanswered questions, and you may come up with even more.

> He stated that after his surgery, he cannot drink anywhere near the amount or volume he used to.

Drink what? How much? Is his stomach smaller, his bladder impaired?

Fortunately, while word choices like these are a bit difficult to decipher, reports written like this are not a very common problem in police reports and can be translated into plain English with a little effort. A more common and more critical problem is using the wrong word.

The suspect vehicle had ensigns burning in an effort to cover the smell of marijuana.

How many graduates of the Naval Academy must you ignite to mask the odor of marijuana?

Perpetrator turned walked away from the front door in a excited manor.

The officer made several errors here, but one is critical. The officer used manor instead of manner. Has anyone ever heard of a "landed estate" getting excited?

"Now, class, is this man lying or laying in the gutter?"

Permission granted by John Callahan/Levin Represents

...observed the complainant wearing red sweatshirt blue pants laying under broken basement steps in basement in sitting position.

Can you spot the two most critical errors in the example above? The easiest to see is the lack of logic. How can a person be lying in a sitting position? By now you should be aware of the second error (remember that lay means to place or set). The officer confused lie and lay and chose the wrong word.

One of the greatest strengths of English is the amazing number of words we can use to get our meaning across accurately and precisely. Unfortunately, this large selection also gives many opportunities for a writer to look foolish. If you have to look up the meaning of the word, don't put it in your report! Take a look at the list below. Each set of words can and is commonly confused. Do you see any old friends on the list?

affect/effect	lie/lay	then/than	its/it's
amount/number	sit/set	weather/whether	their/there/they're
less/fewer	to/two/too	where/were	your/you're
	are/our		

Of course, this list is not complete by any means. It does, however, contain some of the most commonly confused words. See the end of this chapter for a more complete list.

Look at the fourth column. Confusion about how to use the ' often leads to using the wrong word. There are really only two places you can use this little critter and be sure you are right. First, use it to show ownership. For example, "The boy's bike," or if you have more than one boy, "The boys' bike." Keep in mind, though, that words like *mine*, *his*, *hers*, *its*, and *yours* show ownership all by themselves; you don't have to add anything. Second, use it to show that things (letters) have been left out. *It is* becomes *it's*; *you are* becomes *you're*, and so on. But if you tend to confuse a shortened word like *you're* with a different word like *your* (meaning you own it), DO NOT USE THE SHORTENED WORD. You cant, uh, can not make these mistakes if you spell all your words out. By spelling everything out, none of us would write sentences like

> You're extra flashlight is in the briefcase.
>
> It's batteries are dead.
>
> New batteries are over they're.

Try it. The sentences then become

> You are extra flashlight is in the briefcase.
>
> It is batteries are dead.
>
> New batteries are over they are.

We've saved the next two word-related errors for last because to explain them, we have to get a bit more technical and use "English terms." Sorry about that. The first of these is a relatively minor error that is very common in spoken English as well as written police reports. All too often "a" is used when "an" should have been used. To use these words correctly you have to know what vowels and consonants are. Remember Miss Fiddich in grade school class? She told you that the vowels were A, E, I, O, and U. They still are. If you remember these five letters, you've got this concept down pat because the consonants are the rest of the letters in the alphabet. The rule is simple; use "an" before a vowel **sound** and an "a" before a consonant **sound**. Which of these two words would you use before the following?

> on __ exam case.

> conducted __ investigation of above perp.

> Perp pulled out ___ SKS rifle.

If you wrote "a SKS rifle," guess what? You're wrong! "But I followed the rules," we hear you screaming. No, you didn't. This is another of those sneaky little rules. Read the rule again. We said before a vowel **sound**. The 'S' in SKS is pronounced as if it were spelled "es." Anytime initials are used as the name or as a shortcut like SKS, NBC, and X-Ray we have a problem. Consonants used this way usually are pronounced with a vowel sound: eSKS, eNBC, or eX-ray. Other consonants sound like consonants: BOLO, DMV, DUI, DWI, and KIA. Be careful.

Look at this sample that we used earlier.

> Perpetrator turned walked away from the front door in a excited manor.

We told you the officer made several errors here, but we only talked about one. Do you see a second one now? Apply the rule. It should be "an excited manner." Why do we have this rule? The answer is simple; we don't know. It's one of those silly rules that you just have to know and follow. Why? Because if you make this type of error, people have a tendency to think that you're not too bright.

Not only is it important to use *a*, *and*, and *the* correctly, you must make sure you remember to include them. We will discuss this more in depth in Chapter 9, but meanwhile, don't make the mistakes that these officers made:

> Both was arrested for discharging a firearm in occupied dwelling and CCW auto.

> northbound on Eastern Ave. at high rate of speed.

> where I performed field test on the subject.

The final word-related error is, quite honestly, an error that did not occur in very many police reports that we reviewed. Nevertheless, it is a very serious type of error that can have tremendous negative impact on your reports, your testimony, and your career. What was it that Rush said? "Words mean something." This meaning, called denotation, is the dictionary definition. If we use words we know, we don't get into any trouble here. But some words also have a great deal of extra meaning attached to them. This extra meaning, called connotation, is the stuff that gets us into trouble. For example, in the '60s when Hannah Barberra created *The Flintstones* cartoon, their theme song included the line, "We'll have a gay old time." The denotation of gay is "happy, lighthearted." Since then, though, our society has attached another definition to the word gay. This new connotation has the potential to put a whole new meaning to the theme song. While this example is not negative, you must remember that most connotation is negative and intended as an insult. The use of words with this extra, negative baggage can greatly offend someone, and unfortunately, give your readers an incorrect impression of you. You may appear bigoted and prejudicial when you are not. For example,

> Property Taken: Rap/Black CDs

In this report, was the officer trying to honestly describe the CDs quickly and efficiently, or did he show subconscious racism? We think it was the former, but some might think it was the latter. What do you think?

When it comes to connotation, there are no set rules. Connotation changes over time. For example, "Sooners" was a derogatory term used to describe thieving land grabbers in 1889. Over time, it has become a recognized, positive term that residents of an entire state use with pride. Others can be positive or negative depending on the circumstances. Gang, lawyer, teacher, or cop are examples. Still others may differ from culture to culture such as fag for cigarette in England or rubber for eraser in Europe. Even the word "kitchen" can have more than one meaning. It can be a place to cook or, for many African-Americans, the back of the neck. While the vast connotations in our diverse society are outside the scope of this book, we suggest you pick up a copy of *Multicultural Law Enforcement: Strategies for Peacekeeping in a Diverse Society* by Shusta, Levine, Harris, and Wong.

Exercises in Proper Word Choice

Can you find the error in word choice?

1. Sergeant Conser then observed a large puddle of water located near the zucchini in the basement. It was unknown if the intruder had caused the water to be splashed out.
2. Sergeant Matson decided to leave the case up to the discrepancy of the Detective Bureau.
3. Corporal Haight observed the perpetrator to be standing in a crowd of people in the hotel cuspidor.
4. Corporal Close upon stopping the vehicle of the accused found a Smith and Wesson .38 model 15 revolver in the waistband of the accused. The accused was asked to produce a valid Indiana permit and produced a valid Illinois permit. The accused was arrested since the Indiana does not have a receptacle agreement with Illinois.
5. She told me she would be happy to consent to the seizure and sign the form.
6. Mr. Fish turned sideways as he rambled through the purse.
7. Writers approached suspects at Barnes and Noble were both were subdued and arrested.
8. I searched the suspects for weapons. Neither had none.
9. Writer observed busted container on back of reporter's work vehicle.
10. Both comp & susp state their always fighting.
11. Complt states she went into the drug store to fulfill prescription.
12. Subject is a W/M 27-32, dark cloths, vehicle a tan/brn Caravan van.
13. Compl stated she was spending the night over perps house.
14. Writer observed walls with large holes thru them.

15. Officers was working a two men unit.
16. Mr. Walker indicated that the mere refusal would cause her to be violated.
17. The plastic bag which had been obtained from Smith consisted of 1.499 gram of marijuana.
18. Motor skills were definitely effected by the amount of alcohol he consumed.
19. Suspect passed out while in route to jail.
20. Officer Dean and I were dispatched to address reference a BNE of a safe.

Commonly Confused Words

accept/except	to receive; to regard as true	but; other than
access/excess	means of entering or exiting	amount over what is enough
advice/advise	opinion about what should be done	suggest; inform
affect/effect	to influence; to change	to bring about a result (verb); result (noun)
a lot/allot	a bunch	to distribute; to give out
allowed/aloud	to be permitted	to say out loud
all together/altogether	everyone as a group	completely
all ways/always	every way; every approach	every time
already/all ready	previously; before	completely prepared
altar/alter	a religious structure	to change; modify
among/between	used with three or more entities	used with two entities
amount/number	used with things which can not be counted—milk, bread	used with things which can be counted—quarts/gallons, slices/loaves
bare/bear	without covering	to carry; to endure; an animal
brake/break	part of a vehicle; slow down; stop	to divide into pieces
breath/breathe	air that is inhaled or exhaled	to inhale or exhale
bring/take	to take with oneself	to take away
buy/by	to purchase	near; not later than; past
canvass/canvas	to examine carefully	heavy coarse fabric
capital/capitol	leading city; money	legislative building
cease/seize	to stop or discontinue	to take
chose/choose	was selected (in the past)	to select (in the present)

Commonly Confused Words (cont.)

Word	Meaning 1	Meaning 2
close/clothes	to shut	garments
coarse/course	rough	direction; unit of study
complement/compliment	company; to complete	to praise; expression of praise
confidant/confident	close friend	self assured
conscience/conscious	sense of right and wrong	aware; alert
council/counsel	group that governs	to give advice
credible/creditable	believable; trustworthy	deserving of praise
deposition/disposition	testimony under oath	mood; temperament; arrangement
desert/dessert	to abandon; barren land	part of a meal
diner/dinner	person eating; type of restaurant	main meal
drug/dragged	chemical substance used to treat diseases or conditions	past tense of to drag
elude/allude	to evade or escape	to make an indirect reference
ensure/insure	to make certain; to guarantee	to take out or issue insurance
farther/further	greater distance (physically)	advance a person or cause
forward/foreword	direction; send on to another address	introduction to a book or report
hanged/hung	to execute	to suspend; to fasten from above
it's/its	contraction of it is	shows possession
less/fewer	used with things which can not be counted—milk, bread	used with things which can be counted—quarts/gallons, slices/loaves
lie/lay	to recline; to relate a falsehood	to put or place something
lose/loose	unable to keep/find; to not win	not tightly fitted

Commonly Confused Words (cont.)

orientation / orientated	familiarization; bearing	to orient
passed/past	to move ahead of	time before now; beyond
close/clothes	to shut	garments
personnel/personal	people employed by organization	relating to individual; private
plain/plane	ordinary; clear	aircraft; tool; level of development
presence/presents	state of being	gifts
principal/principle	most important; sum of money; head of a school	rule; standard
rise/raise	to stand up or move upward	to move something up
scene/seen	location; public display of strong feeling or emotion	past participle of see (we have seen)
sit/set	to take a sitting position	to place something
special/especially	not ordinary	particularly
stationary/stationery	not moving	writing paper and envelopes
then/than	at that time; in that case	used to make comparison
through/threw	to enter one side and exit the other	past tense of throw
trustee/trusty	member of a board	convict granted special privileges; meriting trust
upon/when	on top of	at what or that time; as soon as
waist/waste	middle of body or garment	to use carelessly; discarded objects
weather/whether	atmospheric conditions	if it is the case that
whole/hole	complete	an opening

Commonly Confused Words (cont.)

who's/whose	contraction of who is	shows possession
you're/your	contraction of you are	shows possession
cite/site/sight	to issue a citation	location	view; vision
fore/for/four	a golfer's warning; situated before	in search of; meant to be received by a specific person	a number between three and five
hour/our/are	unit of time	shows possession	state of being
quiet/quite/quit	without noise	completely; actually	stop; cease
their/they're/there	shows possession	contraction of they are	in that place
to/too/two	toward; in the direction of	also; in addition; excessive	a number between one and three
vein/vain/vane	blood vessel	excessively proud	weathervane
where/ were /we're	at or in a place	a form of to be	contraction of we are

Chapter 7

Comma Man to the Rescue

You are creating reports that will form the basis for critical decisions. Sometimes the pressures on you when you are writing seem unreasonable. You are expected to convey information accurately, clearly, concisely, completely, objectively, and correctly—all with 30 minutes left in your shift and six calls holding.

You've got your audience. You've got the *Who Did What To Whom*. Your kitchen has been removed from your victim's anatomy. You know what you wrote. It's what you meant. But you are still not quite ready to submit the report. You have to use punctuation and use it correctly in your report. There are no exceptions.

Independent clause; dependent clause; independent clause marker; subordinate marker; coordinating conjunction. AAAH! Does correctly punctuating your writing seem like one of the great mysteries of the universe? If your answer is yes, you are not alone. In grade school, in middle school, in high school, in college and/or the academy, you have been given punctuation rule after punctuation rule. Directions like, "This rule is always followed, except when...." How can it be a rule which always applies when there are so many exceptions? Trying to understand punctuation can be difficult, and it may even seem harder than trying to understand court rulings. It shouldn't be, though.

Punctuation is little more than a system for telling your readers how to proceed. Think of punctuation as the traffic signs on the report highway. Wrong sign, no sign, or misplaced sign will result in a fatal accident. Your meaning will be DOA and no amount of emergency treatment can save it. We are going to reduce all the rules into five or ten (thousand). Seriously, police reports will usually be limited to the following basic punctuation marks: periods, commas, semi-colons, colons, quotes, and question marks. You may have noticed that parentheses (), dashes (—), and exclamation points (!) are missing from the list. (A categorical rule— Don't Use Them!)

Take a look at the following section of an officer's report.

> Dahlinger was issued a copy of the breath results his Michigan driver's license was confiscated and he was issued the Michigan temporary driving permit and he was also issued citation 32410 for drunk driving driver failing to wear a seatbelt and a waivable citation for the headlight being out.

This wasn't quite what the officer actually wrote. The officer knew enough about punctuation to realize that something needed to be put in to help the reader understand the report. Comma Man came to the rescue. What the officer actually wrote was

> Dahlinger was issued a copy of the breath results, his Michigan driver's license was confiscated, and he was issued the Michigan temporary driving permit, and he was also issued citation 32410 for drunk driving, driver failing to wear a seatbelt, and a waivable citation for the headlight being out.

While the commas help, there has been a serious accident involving meaning. Some parts of the meaning are in critical condition, while some are DOA. The officer put yield signs at the intersections instead of stop signs. You can pretty much figure out what this officer was trying to say, but by putting in the proper road signs, the meaning becomes clear and can be interpreted only one way.

> Dahlinger was issued a copy of the breath results. His Michigan driver's license was confiscated. He was issued the Michigan temporary driving permit. He was also issued citation 32410 for drunk driving. He was also issued citation 32410 for driver failing to wear a seatbelt. He was also issued a waivable citation for the headlight being out.

The complete thoughts are now marked with stop signs—periods. But, as we saw in Chapter 4, using too many stop signs can make a narrative sound like a first grade reader or a Tarzan movie. Sometimes, merging ideas using ", *and*" makes the information presented read much smoother. This allows your reader to process your information more easily.

> Dahlinger was issued a copy of the breath results, his Michigan driver's license was confiscated, and he was issued the Michigan temporary driving permit. He was issued citation 32410 for drunk driving and for driver failing to wear a seatbelt. He was also issued a waivable citation for the headlight being out.

Now that you understand how to use periods and commas perfectly, we can move onto another punctuation mark. OK? NO. It's clear as mud. Let's take punctuation one mark at a time.

The Period. Stop signs go at intersections. Periods go at the intersections of thoughts and ideas. They tell your reader to stop briefly before continuing. Put a period after a complete thought. Simple sentences convey a complete thought. They stand alone. It should be readily apparent to you that the *Who*, the *Did What*, and the *To Whom* are there. How do you know if it is a complete thought? The acid test is to ask yourself the following question: If someone approached you and used the sentence, would you know what they were talking about or would you call the regional psychiatric hospital and EMS?

> Gave me a list of the stolen property.

Notice that there is no *Who*. There is only a *Did What To Whom*. The thought is not complete. We have to add a *Who*.

> Mrs. Who gave me a list of the stolen property.

Now we have a complete thought or idea. We have a *Who Did What To Whom*.

Sometimes we have a *Who Did What To Whom*, but the thought is incomplete. Apply the acid test to the following example:

> After I made contact with the victim, Jack Bogema, at the Dairy Queen on East 21st Avenue.

If someone approached you, said this, and walked off, would you have any idea what he was talking about? No. This is not a complete thought. Something happened either before or after this sentence, so it needs to be joined to the sentence before it or be told in the sentence after it. A comma can accomplish this, and after you read the next section, it should be an easy fix.

The Comma. Comma Man can come to the rescue when you want to merge a number of actions or items. While the following sentence is correct,

> The suspect went to the back of the store. The suspect entered a red Nissan. The suspect fled the area.

it is quicker to write and easier to read if you use commas.

> The suspect went to the back of the store, entered a red Nissan, and fled the area.

(By the way, there is another error in this sentence. Can you identify it?)

Sometimes you want to merge larger pieces of information, adding a second or third idea to make your report easier to read. Comma Man can again come to the rescue.

> I was unable to obtain a blood sample. I did attempt to procure a search warrant. Mr. Dahlinger was taken to get CAT scans. A blood sample could not be taken.

This is a series of closely related ideas. While all the sentences can stand alone, they produce choppy, isolated ideas. Combine them and they are easier to read and understand.

> I was unable to obtain a blood sample from Mr. Dahlinger. I did attempt to procure a search warrant, Mr. Dahlinger was taken to get CAT scans, a blood sample could not be taken.

The comma now combines all the ideas, yet the sentence is still incorrect. In fact, the proper grammatical term for what we have now may help; it is WRONG. Commas are too weak to hold complete thoughts together by themselves. Just like epoxy glue (or binary explosives), you need Part A and Part B. Part A is the comma. Part B is any **one** of the following words: and, but, or, for, nor, so, or yet. Use both parts.

> I was unable to obtain a blood sample from Mr. Dahlinger. I did attempt to procure a search warrant, but Mr. Dahlinger was taken to get CAT scans, and a blood sample could not be taken.

Commas, however, are strong enough to glue an incomplete thought to a complete thought. Let's go back to our victim, Mr. Bogema.

> After I made contact with the victim, Jack Bogema, at the Dairy Queen on East 21st Avenue.

We said that this incomplete thought needs to be connected to a complete thought. If we connect it to a complete thought that follows it, we get

> After I made contact with the victim, Jack Bogema, at the Dairy

> Queen on East 21st Avenue, I learned that the suspects were driving a yellow Pinto hatchback.

If you want to attach this to the complete thought before it, an odd rule comes into play. Words like after, although, because, since, when, and where are "sticky words." They don't need Part A of the epoxy when they come after a complete thought. For example:

> I learned that the suspects were driving a yellow Pinto hatchback after I made contact with the victim, Jack Bogema, at the Dairy Queen on East 21st Avenue.

Semi-Colon. Semi-colons in police reports should be about as common as fur on frogs. There is one place, however, that they can come in handy. If you have a list of items with additional detail, you must punctuate it correctly or it becomes confusing. If you don't use any punctuation at all, it looks something like this:

> Complainant returned home and stated that the following items are missing: Pioneer CD Changer value $400.00 Kenwood tuner value $500.00 27 inch Panasonic TV value $500.00.

Use only commas and it will look like this:

> Complainant returned home and stated that the following items are missing: a Pioneer CD Changer, value $400.00, a Kenwood tuner, value $500.00, a 27-inch Panasonic TV, value $500.00.

It is difficult to tell which goes with which. Use semi-colons and your reader knows just what goes with what.

> Complainant returned home and stated that the following items are missing: a Pioneer CD Changer, value $400.00; a Kenwood tuner, value $500.00; and a 27-inch Panasonic TV, value $500.00.

Colons. Notice in the burglary report above that a colon was used before the list. Look closely and you will see that each list was introduced by a complete thought and then the colon. When introducing a list in your report, use a complete thought and a colon. Remember, a complete thought is a *Who Did What to Whom.*

At the beginning of your shift, you must check the following equipment: your firearm, leather, handcuffs, and body armor.

If you do not have a *Who Did What to Whom*, don't use a colon before your list.

At the beginning of your shift, check your firearm, leather, handcuffs, and body armor.

Quotes. There will come a point in your report where your description of events is better served by a direct quote from a victim, witness, or suspect. When you choose to use the "exact" words, alert your reader to that fact. Make it clear that the words are not yours but belong to the person who actually said the words. The traffic sign used to indicate this is the quotation mark. However, only use quotation marks to indicate the EXACT statement, not your summary of what was said. Sometimes, a quote is best.

From the Street Cop

When I was a sergeant, one of my officers was a very senior patrolman named Al. One day, Al took a report from a woman who had been raped by a man (why it is necessary to explain this will become obvious in a moment). In Al's report, which, by the way, was one very long sentence, Al said, "At this point, the victim said that the suspect forced her to perform cunnilingus on him." I spoke to Al about this, and told him, "I don't think this is anatomically possible." Al got quite upset, sure that he had used the correct word, and was very frustrated that he had used a word that describes the same basic act, but with the genders reversed. He told me that the victim had told him, "He made me go down on him." I told Al, in the future, that he might be better off just using the quote from the victim, as (1) everyone who reads the report will know what you mean by "go down," and (2) just in case the victim did mean something else, the error in interpretation won't be the officer's.

We have a heck of a problem here. Rather than simply quote the victim, this officer chose to summarize what he thought she said. As a result, he lost a powerful piece of testimony. Exact quotes from the victim, subject, or witness are extremely persuasive and should be used whenever possible. Quotes not only convey the exact feelings and the intensity of the situation in which the statement was made, but they can also be used at trial to impeach a witness who chooses to change his testimony. Quotes are not the result of your interpretations — summaries are.

From the Prosecuting Attorney

Describe the demeanor of the victim and witnesses. If a victim, witness or suspect is excited, hysterical, crying or still suffering from the stress of the crime, any statements made may be allowed into evidence through the testimony of the officer. These statements should be placed in quotations in the police report. These statements become crucial if the victim or witness fails to appear for trial (which occurs frequently in domestic violence situations). Knowing the demeanor of the individuals involved allows the

Prosecutor to understand the situation that the officers were dealing with at the time.

There are many ways to use quotation marks, but cops only need to know two simple ways to quote someone. KISS it. First the quote is followed by who said it; or second, who said it is followed by the quote.

"No," he stated.   or   He stated, "No."

Officers usually make two mistakes when using quotes. The first is placing the end punctuation mark outside of the quote. For example:

He stated, "No".   or   "No", he stated.

The second mistake is quoting something that is not a quote, or not placing quotes around something that is a quote. Take a look at these alleged quotes.

He said that he "sort of" grabbed her.

He said I sort of grabbed her.

The problem with the first example, besides being vague as to what the term *sort of* means, is that the officer could not make up his mind whether or not to use an exact quote. In the second, the officer made up his mind to quote, but failed to do so properly leaving the reader to decide whether the suspect or the officer grabbed her. Properly fixed, they should look something like this:

He said that he sort of grabbed her.

He said, "I sort of grabbed her."

Note that in the second example there is no question that the suspect is trying to minimize his action, whereas in the first example it is unclear whether or not the officer is offering an opinion. Is the officer using slang to convey an idea? We are not sure. KISS it. Don't leave any question about *Who Did What To Whom.*

Question marks. Question marks are only used in offense or incident reports when they are part of an exact quote. They may be used to request an action or an answer in a memorandum, an administrative report, or a letter. In either case, though, be sure that you place a question mark after an actual question. In the following example, the officer thought that she had written a question and ended it with a question mark.

Ron stated that he dashed up to her and asked what she was doing there?

This is not a question. It is a statement. It should have read

> Ron stated that he dashed up to her and asked what she was doing there.

If the witness had stated it as a question, the officer should have written

> Ron stated that he dashed up to her and asked, "What were you doing there?"

Exercises

The following sentences contain numerous errors in punctuation and structure. Try to fix them.

1. Wrts while on routine patrol on Truckenmiller Rd.
2. Salvator stated Trautman provoked Davis, then Davis choked Trautman, then Trautman got a butter knife for his own protection.
3. So bad that the smell was coming into his house.
4. Kay worked there for two days but quit last night, she was the only suspect that Stratton had.
5. I contacted the resident Brooks who stated that he did not have the bike, I asked Rutledge if I could search the Apartment and he agreed verbally.
6. Parrish reported that he looked out the window and he saw that his van window had been smashed out and he called 911.
7. From my previous training and experience as an undercover narcotics officer, I felt that Jesse was indicating that her father smoked marijuana and that the marijuana was in the tin which she was holding, I took the tin from her and opened it.
8. West told me that he saw toward the end of the accident, and thought that Hall was in the inside curb lane, the other vehicle came repidly on the inside where she struck him and then shot off over the curb and down that lane.

9. Officer Rush told me that Deputy Snerdley also photographed the interior of the residence, see his supplement report for additional information.

10. Located inside the suspect vehicle in plain view was two firearms one SKS rifle and a .380 semi auto handgun.

11. Upon speaking to her, it seemed apparent that she had trouble listening following my directions and had trouble remembering what I asked for.

12. I asked him several times about these purchases, and it appeared to me that he was unvaivering in his story and very accurate and articulate about how many bottels of alcohol were purchased and in what manner and fashion they were bought, and how many tot.

13. He said that he was old and weak and he did not see well, and that if she was "messing with him" that was his recourse.

14. I then placed him in handcuffs with his hands behind his back and double locked them and placed him in the rear of my patrol car without incident.

15. One of the A/M struck victim in the living room and they tore up the living room and fled scene.

16. The victim had been taken to the hospital by family members for treatment so the photographes are not fresh wounds but treated wounds.

17. The plate was improper the vehicle was a white/gray four door Crown Victoria with two hispanic males occupancy.

18. But, B/M grabbed the money out Smiths hand , Smith threw beer bottle at the B/M suspect, and Smith fled on foot.

19. Custer said he was kicked in the head and struck with "something" he did not know what, Custer had glass in his hair.

20. When complt notified Yellow Cab Company she was informed no purse had been found.

21. Perp became angry and hit compl on the left eye with his fist and then he threw a marble ashtray and hit compl on the back of her head.

22. Once the reading was completed I informed him that he was under arrest for Minor-Ubal at approx 0335.

23. Both vehicles were southbound on North South Street from West East Street, when vehicle #1, driven by J. P. Sartre and vehicle #2, driven by F. Nietzsche, collided.

24. As I followed the vehicle from the 3400 block of East Chicago to Columbia Road I observed it swerving slightly within its lane.

25. Complt states while he attempted to talk to a friend of his on the street, while still inside his veh. perp started to state: "I'll make you disappear".

26. Wrtrs ordered Jones into the unit to which she responded " Do I have to?"

27. R/O asked if he struck her?

28. I asked Dean where this occurred in the house?

29. A short time later Ms. Kravitz arrived and stated "thats my purse, and thats the guy who stole it", while pointing to Mr. Meier.

30. As compl stated that's him.

31. Wearing a yellow pants outfit, followed her around the store continueously until she obs that her wallet was missing.

32. Complt states while she was shopping at the value Village Market

33. Compl. states she sustained swollen jaw scratches on left arm reddness around throat.

34. This date and time, compl. obs. # 1 on her front porch, compl. refused to let # 1 in, # 1 threw a childs bike thru her frt room window, 3 x 2' window.

35. Upon arr., wrt.'s talked to abv. compl. Who stated that as he was walking on 14th S/B at Gittings Pl when he was approached by the abv. unk. 3 B/M's.

36. As I and my Partner P.O. Patton #1945 were escorting #1 back to the Lockup #1 Began fighting with the compl and his Partner.

37. Writer t/t compl. Who stated perp drove up on him in a gld Geo Metro exited the veh. and produced a lg. knife.

38. T/t pro who stated she had compl's veh at abv loc, when unk person's broke the driver side window of his 90 Plym. white 98 MD abc123.

39. Upon. inv. outer perimeter of house. Wrt & ptr obs side door open & security bars removed from rear window window open.

40. At abv. time/loc. abv subj was adv., arr wrt. conveyed subj to cen. bkg.

41. Above date, time, location, wtr standing at bar w/wife Wilma F. Ruble, T/T bartender: Rebecca Malone W/F; and customere: Norm Clayben W/M when arr. sub. entered began speaking abusively to bartender; demanding to be served at one point screaming "Bitch gimme a fucking drink" wtr asked "sub. to calm down and watch his language".

42.   Wtr and PO. Kirby in the area of the abv loc obs unk B/M look in the dir of wtr and walk into the abv loc, wtr and PO. Kirby exit veh and invt same, wtr knock and annoucne, front door was not lock, wtr obs the abv defts standing in the kitchen area wtr ask for I.d. neither had none, wtr adv the abv defts of rights and place same under arr for the abv chg, convey to the station, the abv loc is has numerous compls of drugs being sold from the side door, and is vacant.

You may have noticed that as the exercises progressed, they became more difficult to understand. At some point in the exercises, figuring out the abbreviations and the shortcuts was harder than the punctuation. Maybe you couldn't even punctuate the sentence because you had no idea what the writer was trying to say. No fun is it? You are a victim of Cop Speak, Abbreviations, and Other Shortcuts.

Chapter 8

Cop Speak, Abbreviations, and Other Shortcuts

The French speak French; the Russians speak Russian; the Americans speak English (although the British strenuously disagree), but what in the heck do cops speak? You work within law enforcement with other cops, and you probably socialize with them when you're off duty. The results are pretty obvious in police reports. Officers tend to talk and write in a dialect of English, a jargon known as Cop Speak. All too often, this dialect is difficult for other English speakers to recognize. This is not a problem in the squad room or over a cup of coffee at Big Apple Bagels™. But when you are communicating with the rest of the world, it can be.

The following sentences are basically okay. The *Who*, *Did What*, and *To Whom* are present in three out of four sentences. Most of the kitchen has been removed from the victim, and each sentence means pretty much what it says. Traffic signs mark the way. So what's wrong with them? Take a closer look. Who is the officers' audience? Probably other cops.

> **From the files**
>
> At this time Bob states he ran out the back door after advising Michael that he was going to call police.
>
> Upon arrival, contact was made with the complainant, Brian Smith, who directed me...
>
> On the below date and time, I contacted an individual for a traffic violation and subsequently conducted an OUIL investigation.
>
> After conducting a traffic stop on a vehicle for an equipment violation, I contacted the driver and immediately detected the odor of intoxicants.

Does anyone really believe that Bob told the officer that he *advised* Michael? How does one make *contact*? Sounds like an encounter with alien life forms. The complainant *directed* me? And how do you *detect* an odor? Did this officer borrow the gas company's sniffer? Cop Speak. The words are used correctly, but do you remember *affray* in Chapter 6? Virtually no one else on the planet uses these words in a conversation, so why do cops want to use them in their reports? Andy Rooney has some thoughts on the subject.

"It's police talk"
by
Andy Rooney

I've been studying a foreign language for the past few weeks. It isn't French, Spanish or Japanese. It's cop talk. The television stations that broadcast the O.J. Simpson trial ought to provide a translator.

If you want to be able to understand what cops say, you ought to learn how to talk their native tongue. To begin with, never call them cops. They call themselves "POLICE OFFICERS."

As a little exercise, translate this sentence into cop talk. Pretend you're on the witness stand.

"I got out of the car, turned left, found the house and walked up to the door where I saw another person."

Here's how [the] sentence would be said by any Los Angeles cop on the witness stand:

"I EXITED the VE-HICK-LE, PROCEEDED NORTH, ASCERTAINED THE LOCATION OF THE RESIDENCE, AND APPROACHED THE ENTRANCE where I OBSERVED another INDIVIDUAL."

From the testimony of the police officers on the stand, I've learned that cars are ve-hick-les, not cars or plain vehicles. Cops never get out of them, they EXIT them. Then, they don't walk, they PROCEED. While they're PROCEEDING, they never simply see something, they OBSERVE it. Nothing is a house, it's THE LOCATION. Doors are always ENTRANCES. Cops don't walk left or right, they PROCEED NORTH or SOUTH.

No one ever comes up to a Los Angeles Police officer.

"Detective Fuhrman APPROACHED me."

"Where did you get the envelope?"

"I OBTAINED THE EVIDENCE from another INDIVIDUAL at the LOCATION." People are never simply men or women, they are INDI-VIDUALS.

"What did he say?"

"The OFFICER SO-IDENTIFIED STATED that he had been AT THE LOCATION for A PERIOD OF ONE HOUR."

"Did you help him?"

"I ASSISTED him in any manner possible."

"Where was the light coming from in the house?"

"The light from the LOCATION was EMANATING from a window on the second floor of the RESIDENCE."

"Did you see someone running away?"

"I OBSERVED the SUBJECT FLEEING ON FOOT FROM THE LOCATION."

"Was he alone?"

"NEGATIVE. He was ACCOMPANIED BY ASSOCIATES AS WE PROCEEDED TO OUR VE-HI-CLE."

"Did you arrest the man?"

"I APPREHENDED the PERPERTRATOR."

I don't know why cops talk this way. We ask a lot of the police. We expect them to be part strong-arm enforcers of the law and part Philadelphia lawyers. We want them to have guns when they need them but we expect them to know all about the Constitution and our laws so they can respect our rights. They're walking a tightrope and it makes them tongue-tied. They resort to familiar, high sounding clichès to give themselves credibility.

Almost every profession has its own special language. In the case of doctors and lawyers, we're all suspicious that they use elaborate, obscurant terms for ordinary things because they want to lose us. It's a deliberate effort on their part to cut us out. They want to make their profession sound harder and more complex than it really is. They use those phrases the rest of us don't understand as a way of making it impossible for us to know what they're talking about.

Cop talk is a way police officers have of lending weight and credibility to their testimony. It doesn't help and they ought to give it up.

Look at the examples again. Rewrite them using common, everyday words. Does your revision have Bob *saying* that he *told* Michael? Did the *I* (the officer) *speak* with the complainant who *told me* (the officer) something? Did you make a traffic stop and then conduct an OUIL investigation? And finally, did you *make* a traffic stop, *speak* with the driver and *smell* the odor? We hope so. Throw the jargon away. Use your thesaurus sparingly or for a door stop. Don't sound like a lawyer wannabe or a stuffy professor. Write for real people.

You can easily avoid Cop Speak if you think about it. Begin by avoiding abbreviations. It is not as easy when you have four reports to finish at the end of your shift. It's all too easy to take the quick way out. The results can look something like

> Writers on r/p w/b w fort at abv loc when obs a blu/85 chevy p/n gw2158 w/b w fort make an inproper lane change w/out signaling.
>
> Unk/B/M/, nfd, driving unk/Chry/4D/Blu, nfd.

Can you figure out what the writers meant? Sure you can, but it may have taken a few minutes to think about some of the abbreviations used, and a non-cop might have had a bit more trouble.

> Comp came into prct on abv day/time & stated
>
> Pro stated she was upstairs,

What is a comp? Is it the same as a compl. or a complainant? The woman in the second example was a Pro. Did the offficer mean a prostitute or person reporting offense? (Other officers in this department use the abbreviation P.R.O.) Remember our goal? Accurate, accessible, clear, concise, complete, and objective communication. Abbreviations may help you be concise and remain objective, but they will do nothing to improve accuracy, accessibility, or clarity.

We are by no means telling you not to use abbreviations. They do have their place in report writing. You should be aware, though, that abbreviations vary within the law enforcement community, across the country, and within a region. They even vary within a department if officers use personal abbreviations rather than standardized ones. Use abbreviations sparingly, and then use only accepted, standardized abbreviations found in a good dictionary or your agency's report writing guidelines.

Cop Speak and abbrns.* are annoying, but more annoying still is the us o shrtcts.** The two most common shortcuts are the *10 Code* and something we call *The subject in box #1*. The *10 Code* was developed for use in **radio** communication and should remain there. Don't use it in written reports unless you are directly quoting another officer. It's too confusing because, like abbreviations, the code varies nationally, regionally, and between agencies. Take a good look at the following piece from the Law Enforcement Forum on CompuServe. Can you translate it?

> SUBJ: 10- CODED Message Section: Police Chatter
> FROM: Paul Nash/VA
> To: All
> DATE: 08/29/92 21:38:13
>
> The other day a 10-20 told me about several 10-78s that were possibly 10-32 with 10-29s. I went 10-12, CODE 3, but was too late. I was unable to locate the 10-61s but was lucky enough to find some 10-80 that some unknown 10-18 must have stashed from a recent 10-45 or 10-53. It's a good thing I had 10-6 or there might have been a 10-1 or 10-13, but everything went 10-4. I took the 10-80 to 10-16 and did a CODE 8 with it. I went back 10-8. The dispatcher said she thought I was on a 10-29 and wanted to know why I was CODE 7 and not CODE 6. I replied, 10-29, what the hell is A 10-29?? There is no such thing. She said she was sorry, it was a typo and changed it back to the original 10-67 message and cleared it CODE 8. Ohh well, another day over with and I'm still alive and in one piece.

At least one officer from Nevada accepted the challenge, and his translation is:

---

* Abbreviations
** Use of Shortcuts

SUBJ: 10- CODED   Message Section: Police Chatter
FROM: Tim Dees/NV
TO: Paul Nash/VA
DATE: 08/30/92 03:08:08

*Just to show you how codes differ from one spot to another,
here's what you said in Reno-ese:* "The other day a 10-20 (location) told me about several 10-78s (officer needs emergency assistance) that were possibly 10-32 (man with a gun) with 10-29s
(inquiry for wanted). I went 10-12(stand by), CODE 3 (red lights
and siren), but was too late. I was unable to locate the 10-61s
(personnel in area) but was lucky enough to find some 10-80
(chase in progress) that some unknown 10-18 (complete assign-
ment quickly) must have stashed from a recent 10-45 (dead ani-
mal) or 10-53 (road blocked). It's a good thing I had 10-6 (busy)
or there might have been a 10-1 (reception poor) or 10-13 (weather or road report), but everything went 10-4 (acknowledged). I
took the 10-80 (chase in progress) to 10-16 (domestic distur-
bance) and did a CODE 8 (arrest record information) with it. I
went back 10-8 (in service). The dispatcher said she thought I
was on a 10-29 (check for wanted) and wanted to know why I
was CODE 7 (meal break) and not CODE 6 (follow up). I replied,
10-29 (wants check), what the hell is a 10-29 (wants check)??
There is no such thing. She said she was sorry. It was a typo and
changed it back to the original 10-67 (go ahead with your traffic) message and cleared it CODE 8 (arrest record information).
Oh well, another day over with and I'm still alive and in one
piece."

Makes a lot of sense, doesn't it?

Just as maddening as the *10 Code* is the *The subject in box #1*. Is the
following segment of a report easily followed and understood? Keep in
mind that you are on page two of the report and the boxes, referred to
as "above" and "below," are actually on the cover sheet and a supplement.

From the typewritten files

Wrts made the above loc obs the above perp whom stated he was the driver of the below listed impounded veh highly intoxacated. As the above perp was receiving medical treatment for a cut to his right thumb he sustained in the motor veh accident. wrts obs the above perp unable to stand on his own slurred speech, blood shot eyes and a strong oder intoxicants emminating off the above perps body. at this point wrts advised an arr the above perp for O.U.I.L. and conveyed him to the second dst for processing. wrts obs the above perp veh with heavy accident damage to the front end.

Wrts also obs a white cup with it's contents spilled over in interior of the above perps veh. The veh also smell of strong intoxicants.

This officer did not resort to the *10 Code,* but he managed to violate all of the other guidelines presented in this chapter, the previous chapters, the remaining chapters, and some we did not think necessary to discuss in this book. Think about what this officer did to all of the readers of this report. When you were in school, did you appreciate textbooks that constantly referred you to another page or an appendix? Of course not. No reader likes the hassle, and flipping pages tends to make readers forget what they were just reading.

The writers of the following reports did not abuse their readers quite so thoroughly. Each of these segments was located on the bottom of the cover sheets. Readers of the first report had to search the top of the sheet to determine the location of the box marked location.

Compl returned to loc and discovered the damages below and the items missing.

CIRC: Pro states unk perp broke the store front window at abv loc on both dates.

The second officer must have a cruel sense of humor. He not only forced the readers to figure out the abbreviations and where the necessary boxes were, but he also compounded the confusion by referring to "both dates" when a three day span was specified in the box.

Like your firearm, Cop Speak, abbreviations, and shortcuts should be used as a last resort.

Exercises

Can you figure these out? They are reproduced exacly as they appeared in the original reports (identifying information has been changed, of course).

1.   WRITERS AT ABV LOC GIVING
2.   Abv. mentioned plus abv. loc. had recently been on fire al of fire damage. Abv subj was under debris. White pants dirty from ashes.
3.   WRTS. AR 2 ABV. LOCATION T/T COMPL. WHO STATED SHE WAS IN HER VEH. A 1992 MASERATI 4-D GREY 99/OK/SNR127 VIN.# ZAMAN2106MB317706 @ THE ABV. LOCATION WHEN HER X-BOYFRIEND ERIC STRATTON B/M/43 OF 171 BONN PULLED UP IN HIS BMW 318 2-D GREY W/ HIS NEW GIRLFIREND & THE ABV. DEF & ONE OTHER BLK FEMALE THE DEF EXITED THE VEH. W/ THE COMPL'S X-BOYFRIEND APPROACHED THE VEH. & STATED "I'M GONNA KILL YOU" THEN STARTED BREAKING OUT THE WINDOWS OF THE COMPL.'S VEH & STRUCK THE COMPL. ONCE IN THE LEFT FOREARM W/ A CROWBAR WHILE THE COMPL.'S X-BOYFRIEND HELD THE DOOR CLOSED.
4.   On Above Dates Complt was in an Acc & Acc Report #6852019 After Acc, Complts veh was towed by West towing. When Complt CKD veh at Tow yard a day later. A number of Items were missing from his veh.
5.   PRO TX TCRU
6.   Wtrs while on R/P obs abv perp at abv add.consume.
7.   At Abv loc, Wro made loc obs 92 Chrysler Lp 1X379 vin # 2C3E56F9RD693621 on fire Also part of pump 2 was on fire.
8.   P/R to Abv loc R/A

Chapter 9

Pruf Reeding or Hookt on Fonix Rilly Wurkt Fer Mee!

Congratulations! Your report is written, and while it won't be nominated for the Nobel Prize in Literature, it won't get kicked back by your supervisor either. Or will it? Now you have to go over what you have written to make sure that it is accurate, accessible, clear, concise, complete, and objective. Oh, we should add one more item to this list of features that all good reports share. They should be CORRECT.

> **From the Undersheriff**
>
> You are what you report. A factually accurate report containing numerous grammatical or spelling errors will not carry the same credibility as a report that "looks good." A sloppy report connotes laziness which in turn may generate suspicions about accuracy. Consequently, it should come as no surprise that supervisors form strong opinions about officer performance based upon report writing skills. In the end, two officers may be equally talented at detecting criminal activity, interviewing suspects and making arrests but the officer who writes excellent reports will likely possess far greater respect and enjoy a much more rewarding career in law enforcement than an officer who doesn't.

We wish that we could tell you there is a machine or computer program that will do this for you. But there isn't. Proofreading thoroughly and well is hard. Impossible? NO. Difficult? YES. Easy? With practice.

Someone, we think it was Alro Guthrie the folk singer/philosopher, once said, "You can't have a light without a dark to stick it in." He could have been talking about proofreading (proofing). The most important tool for proofing is knowing the weaknesses in your own writing. Each of us has our own unique set of writing errors. Do you spell porely? Tend to write fragments rather than complete thoughts? Do your detail "bullets" always seem to miss the center of mass? Perhaps you use too many

short cuts or too much Cop Speak. Each of us has our own unique set of errors. Don't just say, "Yup, and I know them when I see them." Remember nothing ever happened unless it is written down. Write down your errors. Keep a list of them in the back of your clipboard; refer to the list before you begin proofing any written report. Update the list frequently because you will soon stop making the basic errors, and you will begin to identify other, more subtle and sophisticated errors to keep your list full. In other words, identify your own dark.

The single most powerful tool for proofing is time. The more time that you can put between drafting your report and proofing it, the better. This is usually easy when you are writing letters, memorandums, or administrative reports. You will probably have the luxury of putting several hours or even days between drafting and proofing. You won't have this luxury when writing incident and offense reports. Why is time so important? Quite simply, your brain will lie to you. You are focused on the report while writing, and you are carrying a copy of the report around in your head. *You* know what you're trying to say, and even if it isn't on the page, your subconscious will say, "Yup. It's all there and lookin' good." Time allows this internal copy of your report to be erased from your mind or at least to be placed into storage.

> **From the Undersheriff**
>
> Investing time is a must. Most police reports focus on answering the proverbial who, what, where, when, how and why. While there is the occasional officer who tends to be too verbose in pursuing this objective, officers are more likely to take shortcuts and leave out information necessary for follow up investigation and prosecution. No one is perfect and human error will always be an issue, but the more common problem is "avoidable error" that comes from being in too much of a hurry to write/dictate a report.

What should you do if you don't have time? The same effect can be achieved if you write two or more reports *before* going back and proofing the first one. Try it. You'll be surprised at the results. Your mind will be carrying around a copy of the third report, and when you reread the first report, you'll see only what is actually on the page, not what you thought was there.

Does your agency still have you writing reports in pen or pencil? You know, only time for one version done under the dome light and that's it. This can be a problem because you obviously won't be able to rewrite the entire report. In this case, add two steps after you've reread your field notes but *before* you actually write the report. Outline the report and reread your list of errors. Then write the report, double checking for the errors you habitually make. This is not as good as using time and rewrites, but with practice, you can make it almost as effective. Time is still your most powerful tool. The few extra minutes spent writing your report will save you and your agency more time. Time that won't be lost due to confusion, questions, and quite possibly lawsuits.

You can no more proof your writing in a single reading than you can complete a complex investigation by speaking to one witness or collecting one piece of potential evidence. You were taught the acronym PRELIMINARY* to use as a framework for an investigation. Use accurate,

---

* Proceed to the scene safely and effectively; Render assistance to the injured; Effect the arrest of the suspect; Locate and identify witnesses; Interview the complainant and the

accessible, clear, concise, complete, objective, and correct as the framework for proofing. The rest of this chapter focuses on the proofing of incident and field reports, but you can easily apply these methods to any other reports you may write on the job.

First, read your report and make sure that it is both complete and accurate. Look over your cover sheet. Are all of the appropriate boxes and blank spots filled in? Do you have each person in the correct box? (Remember the "dead" complainant and live victim?) Check all of the facts against your field notes. Are your facts accurate? Did you spell people's names correctly? Once you are sure that your cover sheet is complete and accurate, check the narrative against your field notes and the cover sheet. They should all match. (Remember our officer in Chapter 8 who mentioned "both days" in the narrative while three days were given on the cover sheet?) Mistakes like this can destroy your reputation and that of the department.

From the Undersheriff

Everyone who plays a role within the criminal justice system basically trusts "if it isn't in the officer's report, it didn't happen." This trust works in favor of the officer until a significant piece of information surfaces that the officer "neglected" to put in the report. Trust then quickly becomes mistrust which one may never recover from. Investing the necessary time to do a complete report will ensure trust is never needlessly damaged.

Second, look your report over to make sure that it is accessible. Remember that some of your readers will not read the report from beginning to end. They will look for only that information necessary for them to do their jobs. Have you used headings and/or subheadings as cues for these readers? If not, consider doing so. Did you start a new paragraph each time you introduced new material or another idea? If not, do so.

Third, check your report for correctness, conciseness, and clarity. This is the longest and most difficult step. You can't read it through once to

---

witnesses; Maintain the crime scene and protect the evidence; Interview the suspect; Note conditions, events, and remarks; Arrange for the collection of evidence or collect it yourself; Report the incident fully and accurately; Yield the responsibility for the investigation to the follow-up investigator.

complete this step. Read your report *backwards* one sentence at a time. Focus. Each sentence must be a complete thought. There must be a *Who*, *Did What*, and a *To Whom*. Your descriptive bullets should be near the center of mass. Your punctuation should be correct. Unnecessary words and phrases should be eliminated. Say what? Sometimes we write like we speak and add words or phrases that are meaningless. Remove all of this extra baggage. The following two examples contain extra words. We've highlighted the unnecessary word in the first example for you. Can you spot the extra baggage in the second example?

> They walked into her front foyer *way* and...
>
> He indicates that they returned back to the residence shortly after 9:00am.

The next two examples contain useless, unnecessary phrases. Can you spot them?

> It was apparent that Mr. Marlow was not wearing his seatbelt, due to the fact the steering wheel was completely collapsed and he did not have it on at the time.
>
> I spoke briefly with the homeowner, that being a Jeff Schmidt.

By the way, according to the report, what else wasn't Mr. Marlow wearing?

The baggage in these two examples is typical of many of the reports we reviewed. Look closely. Why did the first officer use the phrase "due to the fact that" when *because* says it more concisely and clearly? He also added "he did not have it on at the time." The officer should have KISSed it. In the second example, the officer added another unnecessary phrase, "that being." Why not just say "...the homeowner, Jeff Schmidt"? Now check for clarity. Read your report from the beginning, but only read every other paragraph. Is each paragraph a clear and logical unit? That is, do they each make sense? If the answer is yes, repeat the process with the paragraphs you skipped. Then read the entire report. Read it out loud if at all possible. Try to visualize the descriptions you included to be sure they are clear. Listen for "ly" words like strangely, viciously, and others that will ruin the objectivity of your report. Listen for words that carry extra meaning and get them out of your report. When you have done all of this, you finally have a report that any law enforcement professional would be proud to sign. Well, not quite. We left out the very last step. Fourth, check your spelling.

To help you, we've included a list of commonly misspelled words at the end of this chapter.

This cartoon and the following poem show exactly why we left out spell checkers and grammar checkers up to now:

"Speed Bump." (c)1997 by Creator's Syndicate, Inc.
Used by permission of the artist.

I have a spelling chequer
It came with my pea sea
It plainly marques four my revue
Miss steaks eye cannot sea.

When iey strike a quay, right a word
I weight four it two say
Weather eye am wrong oar wright
It shows me strait aweigh

As soon as a mist ache is maid
It nose bee fore two late
And eye can put the error rite
Its rarely, rarely grate.

I've run this poem threw it
I'm shore your please two no
Its letter perfect in it's weigh
My chequer tolled me sew.

Our experience with them is that they are excellent TOOLS, but it is not a good idea to RELY on them. They will not tell you when a properly spelled word is really the wrong word. Remember *Your* and *You're*? They will not tell you when you have used an alternate spelling such as

British	American
offence	offense
theatre	theater
harbour	harbor
grey	gray

And they won't tell you when you have used a word that hasn't been used in our country in over a century, at least as long as you spell the word correctly. Remember affray? We have found that spelling and grammar checkers may also suggest changes that are incorrect. In fact, grammar checkers are now politically correct and will suggest using a gender neutral word like "one" when you are referring to complainant who is a he or a she. Instead of "She said this" you get "One said this." For those of you who use computers for report writing, use your spelling and grammar checkers after *you* complete and proof your report. For fun, try opening the file again and accepting all of the suggestions the checkers made. Is it what you really meant?

We have three suggestions for a final check of your report. Have your partner or another officer read it. Does it make sense to her? Second, as you struggle to complete reports, save a copy of the best ones you've written. Keep one good report of each type (robbery, assault, accident, burglary, etc.) in your briefcase. Use them as templates for calls of a similar nature. They will serve as both a check and a reinforcement. Finally, develop your own report writing checklist. At the end of this chapter, we've given you a couple. Use them as a starting point.

Remember,

From the Street Cop

"Police Reports Are Forever."

Sample Checklists

From the Prosecutor

DOMESTIC VIOLENCE INVESTIGATION CHECKLIST
___ Address, date and time of incident
___ Name, race, DOB, address, home and work telephone of:
    a) Victim
    b) Suspect
    c) Witnesses, including children
___ Relationship of victim and suspect
___ Relationship of any witness to victim or suspect
___ PPO, conditional bond, probation or parole order documented
___ Name of person who called police, if call was to 911, and dispatcher who took call

___ Whether alcohol/drug use was involved and by whom
___ Narrative describing the-incident and scene, describing:
  a) Incident and what led up to it
  b) Whether and how many times the suspect physically assault-
     ed the victim
  c) Description of weapons, object, and or firearm used
  d) Description of all injuries sustained by the victim, and how they
     occurred
  e) Description of all injuries sustained by the suspect, and how
     they occurred
  f) If medical attention was sought: how victim was transported,
     if victim was admitted to hospital, name and other pertinent
     information on ambulance and medical personnel
  g) A description of any property damage reported or evident at
     scene
  h) Facts to support all elements of any offenses committed
  i) Spontaneous utterances made at the scene
  j) A description of the demeanor and emotional state of the per-
     son making the spontaneous statement
  k) Documentation of evidence collected at the scene
  l) Document rationale for arrest or no arrest decision. If suspect
     is not arrested, document efforts to locate suspect
  m) Document if victim was given a Victim Rights Card and refer-
     rals made
  n) If victim seeks shelter, document victims location on a memo and
     attach to report
  o) Previous history of domestic violence
  p) Date, time, name, badge number and signature of reporting
     officer
___ Document lethality factors
___ Document FIA notification when there is a child victim or witness

VICTIM

___ Interview the victim
___ Describe victim's location upon arrival
___ Administer first aid to victim
___ Describe victim's injuries in detail

___ Record excited utterances made by victim
___ Describe victim's emotional condition
___ Describe victim's physical condition
___ Document victim/suspect relationship
___ Document previous history of abuse
___ Document if PPO/bond conditions/probation or parole order exists
___ Give the victim a Victim Rights card and explain rights
___ Record any temporary address/telephone on a memo and attach to case
___ Document evidence of alcohol/drug use

SUSPECT

___ Interview the suspect
___ Describe suspect's location upon arrival
___ Administer first aid to suspect
___ Describe suspect's injuries in detail
___ Record excited utterances made by suspect
___ Describe suspect's emotional condition
___ Describe suspect's physical condition
___ Document evidence of alcohol/drug use

WITNESS

___ Interview reporting party
___ Identify and interview all witnesses separately
___ List names, DOB and other pertinent information of children present
___ Interview children
___ Lists names and other pertinent information of ambulance, and medical personnel

EVIDENCE

___ Identify if call came in on 911, who made call to police, and the dispatcher who took the call
___ Photograph or diagram of crime scene
___ Photograph victim injuries Photograph suspect injuries
___ Photograph or collect torn clothing
___ Impound all firearms/weapons used
___ Impound firearms for safe keeping
___ Attach related reports, photographs

From the Use of Force Expert

USE OF FORCE REPORT CHECKLIST

____ **Initial Assessment:** Fully describe your observations of the scene and the individual(s) involved. Include the nature of the call; whether you were dispatched to the call, flagged down by someone, or you initiated the contact; the location and time of the incident; whether you arrived in a marked or unmarked car; whether you were in uniform; what you saw, heard, smelled; and, what was learned from others on the scene.

____ **Approach:** Fully describe how you approached the individual based on your observations. Include verbal instructions or commands you gave to gain compliance. Fully explain all verbal communications employed with the individual throughout the entire incident, regardless of whether they were followed.

____ **Individual's Response:** In order to justify a level of force, you must predicate your force decision making on the resistive actions of the person. Therefore, you must provide a full description of the appearance, body language, behaviors, verbal responses, and physical resistive actions of the individual. Describe in detail any weapons the person may have possessed/used, or were at his disposal, including your weapon. In order to more fully describe an individual's actions, you are encouraged to refer to your department's use of force policy and a force continuum when you complete this section.

____ **Your Response:** In this section, you should completely describe your response to the individual's resistance. Assisted by the force continuum and policy, you should chronologically explain the escalation/de-escalation control methods used in controlling the person. Fully describe methods of verbal strategies employed (or attempted), all empty-hand and force equipment utilized, and that the person was handcuffed, the handcuffs were double locked, and the individual was searched prior to transport. If an aerosol was applied fully document how may bursts were used, from what distance, its effect, the decontamination procedures utilized, the monitoring protocol, and all complaints voiced by the person. Fully document any injuries that were sustained by the person, if medical assistance was offered, if the person declined or accepted the treatment offered, medical assistance you provided, whether emergency medical personnel were summoned or whether you transported the person to a medical facility. Describe any injuries you sustained and whether the injuries required treatment/hospitalization.

___ **Transport Procedure:** This final section provides a detailed account of the person's demeanor, actions, verbalizations, and complaints you observed during transport. Include the duration of the transport, how the individual was transported, where the person was transported, and how the transport decision was made.

Commonly Misspelled Words

accelerator
acquire
administered
alcoholic
a lot (2 words)
aluminum
ammunition
amphetamine
annual
antiseptic
appearance
apprehended
approximately
arguing
argument
arouse
assault
assistance
available
balloon
bedspread
beginning
believe
belligerent
benefit
Benzedrine
beverage
bicycle
booze
brassiere
bureau
burglary
calendar
candidate
carburetor
caught
cellophane
circular
claim

cocaine
Codeine
coercion
coherent
coincidence
coming
commission
commit
committing
companion
complaints
complainant
concerning
concert
conscious
continuously
controlling
conversation
cooperation
corpse
counterfeit
criminal
cushion
defecate
defendant
definite
definitely
delinquency
delinquent
description
desperate
deterrent
Dexedrine
dilated
directly
discrepancy
disposed
disregard
dosage

drunken
drunkenness
effect
employment
en route
entirely
entitled
environment
epilepsy
epileptic
erratic
evening
exaggerate
excellent
experience
expired
explanation
familiar
familiarize
fascinate
feces
feminine
fictitious
finally
forcibly
forcing
fraudulent
funeral
further
gardener
generous
governor
grievance
gymnasium
handkerchief
hanger
happiness
height
heroin

Commonly Misspelled Words (continued)

hitchhiking	loose	patience
homicide	louver	patient
hygiene	lying	patrolled
hypodermic	machine	peddler
illegal	machinist	penis
illegitimate	maintenance	perform
improvement	manifest	personal
inability	marijuana or	personnel
inadequate	marihuana	perspiration
incapable	marital	perspire
incoherent	marriage	phony
indefinite	masculine	physician
independence	maybe	pneumonia
indict	measles	pornographic
institution	merchandise	possession
interest	minimum	prejudice
interrogate	miscellaneous	premise
interrogated	mischievous	prescription
intersection	months	presence
intoxication	morgue	principal
investigate	municipal	principle
investigation	necessary	probable
involved	night	procedure
irrelevant	numerous	proceed
jewelry	obedience	proceeded
judgment	obedient	profane
jurisdiction	occasion	profession
juvenile	occasionally	progressive
knives	occurred	prominent
knowledge	occurrence	prosecutor
knuckles	odor	psychopathic
lawyer	offense	pursue
leave	opposition	pursuit
liaison	panicked	quantity
license	parallel	quarantine
lieutenant	paraphernalia	quarreling
lights	partial	quiet
liquor	partially	ransacking
lose	passenger	receipt

receive	shiny	themselves
received	shortly	thorough
receptacle	signaled	together
reciprocal	similar	tonight
recommend	simulate	traffic
reference	solicit	translate
register	solicitor	trespass
registration	souvenir	twenties
repetition	squirrel	unconscious
respectfully	statutory	uncontrollably
response	straight	unkempt
restaurant	straightening	vacation
revealed	stupor	vaccinate
rhythm	subpoena	vengeance
river	substance	verbatim
sabotage	substantiate	verified
saliva	substitute	verify
scene	succeed	vial
screams	succeeded	violator
security	successful	visible
seized	successfully	wanted
sentence	suicide	warrant
separate	surveillance	willful
separated	suspicion	willfully
separately	swerved	writing
sergeant	tentative	written
several	tequila	
sheriff	terminal	

Exercise

If you are currently an officer, pull some of your old reports. If you are not, find some of your writing. Identify your own dark.

Chapter 10

A Look Ahead

Technology is making great strides in *assisting* you in your report writing efforts. It does not replace your ability to report accurately, accessibly, clearly, concisely, completely, objectively, and correctly. There is an old saying: Garbage In, Garbage Out. No amount of technology can replace your ability to communicate correctly. Attesting to this fact are the many reports that we have used here that were typed, dictated, or computer generated.

Our next focus box was written by Edward P. Edwardson, Chief of the Wyoming, Michigan, Police Department. The Wyoming Police Department has been chosen by Lucent Technologies as a premier technology site in Michigan and is in the process of converting its infrastructure to the latest technological tools. The Chief is a former board member of the Michigan Law Enforcement Officer's Training Council and currently is on the board of Michigan Futures, an economic think tank. He offers some personal thoughts and observations about the future of report writing.

From the Chief

POLICE REPORT WRITING IN THE 21st CENTURY

There can be no doubt that the methods currently utilized by the police to gather, record, and disseminate various information during the course of their work will dramatically change as we usher in the new millennium.

Certainly we can reasonably expect the rapidity of change relative to technology to continue unabated into the new century. Ideas beget ideas. Change is a constant, and we need to become as adaptive as possible. The most intriguing current technology under research and development is that of voice recognition. Using this technology, officers will be able to dictate their various reports and have the transcriptions done automatically by specialized software which can translate speech into text. Once this is accomplished, departments could utilize report formats,

123

spell/grammar checks, etc., to create the "perfect" police report—or could they?

We are not far away from the perfection of this technology. Indeed, personal versions of this technology are available for purchase today and affordable versions are on the horizon. At issue, though, are not the technological possibilities. This software will present an incredible possibility to create more duty time to problem solve our community's crime issues if it is utilized professionally. Unfortunately, although we may achieve a way to turn speech into text, the software still will only print out what the officer speaks.

A police report that today is incomplete, not concise, unintelligible, etc. will retain the same negative characteristics in the new system. Technology will, however, significantly speed up our ability to complete a bad police report.

So where do we go with police report writing? How do we improve them? It seems to me there are several possibilities.

First, police administrators/managers need to seriously review the whole spectrum of police report issues. They must demonstrate leadership and vision by asking some very tough questions. What do we really need to report? What are we using the information for? How can we improve intra-organizational access and dissemination of information contained in reports? How can we automate the process? What technologies are available to assist us in quality assurance areas?

Police departments need to re-examine these types of issues to be able to construct the necessary foundation upon which they can begin the essential report writing shift from quantitative to qualitative. How can we eliminate unnecessary reports to provide the additional time to prepare those serious, complex, or critical incident reports in a thorough, concise, and professional manner?

More specifically, we need to rethink our reporting requirements to non-criminal/service rendered types of calls. The creation of computer aided dispatch systems coupled with automated number identification (ANI) or automated location identification (ALI) make it possible for us to create built in code menus that officers/dispatchers can function key from in-station or in-car mobile data terminals or personal computers. A significant number of calls for service could be reported through this method. A record of call receipt, call response, action taken, and call status could be accomplished simply, efficiently, and electronically. Using methods such as this will provide the additional time to achieve the quality reporting required in arrests, serious personal injury cases, complex felonies or other major criminal incidents.

We can not and should not become reliant on technology to solve our report writing problems. There must always exist a basic understanding of what a good police report needs to contain. Our reports need to be based on thinking that produces information formatted in a logical, concise, thorough, yet brief, manner. If we want to sustain the formal charges we seek to levy against a defendant, we must present a case that contains all of the necessary information from criminal elements to witnesses to evidence to incriminating statements, etc.

We can mechanically require an officer to do these things through technology. But what happens when the officer is sworn in to testify before a court of law about his/her report? Report writing is an essential skill, which must be mastered by all officers. If you have already mastered these skills, congratulations. If you haven't, your department needs to provide the remedial help you need. More importantly, you as a police officer have a significant professional responsibility to acquire and utilize those skills.

This book was written using the latest in electronic and media technology. We received e-mail submissions from departments, FAXed copies back and forth, wrote on laptop and desktop computers, printed drafts on laser printers, electronically scanned in articles, submissions, and cartoons, and used spell checkers and grammar checkers. Still, all this technology did not *write* the book. The technology simply made it *easier* to write the book. The contents are our responsibility and we, along with those who contributed to it, take the credit. We alone take full responsibility for any errors or omissions. This book, like your police report, is a human product subject to all those frailties of the human condition. We have in this book, like you will do in your reports, taken great care to ensure that it is correct and free of errors. We have reviewed it, proofread it, asked others to proofread it, and edited it many times. If this sounds familiar, it is. We use the same techniques in our writing that we suggest you use in yours. While you may feel a bit overwhelmed with all the rules and guidelines, take heart. The more you apply the principles contained here, the better your written reports will become.

From the Sergeant*

Officers who decide on their own to begin writing clear, simple reports in plain English should not expect that their supervisors will automatically be struck by the brilliance of their innovation. Bosses, and particularly police bosses, can be captives of tradition. If they were taught to write jargon-filled police reports when they began their careers, they may persist in the belief that that style is correct. Your simpler reports may be unappreciated by such hidebound supervisors. You have to do what your bosses tell you, but don't let that stop you from innovating. You can have a profound effect on your department purely by your own example. Let me give you an example:

My department (a large suburb that borders Chicago) has two roll calls for each watch, so that half of the patrol force remains on the street while the other half changes shifts. When I was a patrol officer listening to supervisors give roll call, I always thought that, while giving us our assignments, they should also read off the assignments for the other half of the shift so we would know who we would be working with. When I made Sergeant, at the first roll call I gave, I did so—and it was the first time it was ever done. In time, all supervisors began following my example, and it has remained a standard part of roll call ever since. I doubt if anyone else on my department is even aware of the change, or who originated it.

The point is that rather than send a recommendation up through the chain of command, where it could have been rejected, I simply made a small innovation in my *own work. In doing so, I* (unintentionally) set an example which others followed. A tradition was changed in a small way without anyone ever really being aware of it, and the department is (slightly) better for it.

---

* Geoff Sjostrom is a sergeant with Oak Park (IL) Police Department.

Your nontraditional reports may not be welcome at first. Write your reports as you are directed, but keep them as simple and clear as you can. Over time, you may find that others emulate your simple style of writing until it permeates your entire organization. You may not receive any recognition for it, but you will have done a good thing for your department.

You can make a difference.

Afterword

Think for a moment about the book you've just finished. You've heard from a lot of people who are interested in your reports and, by now, we hope you see them as more than just documents used by a very limited number of people. You probably noticed some common ideas that each of our contributors shared. Our final contributor is another member of your audience. Currently with a major television network, Loren Gold-farb is an investigative journalist and has worked for two major metropolitan newspapers: one in the west, and one in the southeast. He shares his thoughts on the importance of well written police reports in a way that truly brings everything in the preceding chapters together.

From the Investigative Reporter

I imagine that when you write a report, whether incident or arrest, your mind's eye sees an audience of only a few: detective, prosecutor, and defense attorney. Perhaps these are the only people to whom you, the officer on the beat, pays much heed.

You listen to criticisms from the detective and prosecutor because, after all, you're all on the same side; you want to lock away the bad guys as much as they do. The defense attorney you tolerate, begrudgingly, because he knows which of your mistakes can help him unravel a prosecutor's case and send his client walking; seeing the bad guy strut out of court back to the streets because of your blunder pains you. So what pearls of wisdom could I, a journalist, add to this stew of advice? Many police officers view journalists as the proverbial thorn in their side. I can't claim not to understand why. We have an insatiable desire for information and often, at least in the case of crime and courts, you're the ones who have it. While you're focusing on today and tomorrow, we're quizzing you about yesterday, the day before, two years ago.

More often than not, the information I gather from police officers comes in conversation, over the phone usually, but sometimes in person. But a police report can also prove an invaluable roadmap for a journalist.

Perhaps I'm looking for patterns of a specific type of crime, say home invasion robbery. I would submit a public record's request to the police Public Affairs office for all reports of home invasion in a specific time frame. The information culled from the reports would tell me how often home invasion happened in that time frame, the average value of the property stolen, and the number of people injured or killed. The reports will undoubtedly contain names of victims (unless local privacy laws require them to be redacted). The narrative written on the report will guide me in selecting the appropriate person(s) to speak with and select for on-camera interviews.

All of this is contingent upon the quality of the police reports. Of course, it's difficult, if not impossible, to judge quality unless you can read the words that are supposed to form it. In my experience, legible handwriting matters just as much as the facts themselves. I hear my grade school teachers and parents laughing as I type these words. My handwriting would not hold up as an example of quality penmanship. Fortunately for me, I do most of my writing with a keyboard. Unfortunately, most police officers are not afforded the luxury of a laptop on which to complete their reports. I'm sure I'm only echoing what has been written by others who've authored essays for this book, so I won't belabor the point: legible handwriting is crucial to deciphering a police report.

Another technical imperative is a forceful pen on paper. Like any form with multiple copies, the last page receives less pressure than the first and so it can be more difficult to read. Often, photocopies for public inspection are made from that last page. If print on the last page is light, you can imagine how faint that writing will be on a copy.

Now let's talk about the information in the report. Never fudge it; always tell the truth. From the ivory tower of a classroom, this statement seems so obvious. But errors, omissions and downright lies do creep into police reports. I recently watched an investigative series produced by a local television station in which the reporter proved officers lied and covered up the truth behind the macing of an unarmed civilian. In their reports, officers claimed they had to subdue a young woman because she was unruly. The officers did not know that someone nearby witnessed the incident and captured it on videotape, which showed an officer macing the suspect *after* she had been handcuffed and, as the officer was about to place her in a cruiser. The tape proved the woman offered no resistance. The reporter contrasted the videotape with reports written by officers at the scene. In short, assume every incident about which you're writing a report will be documented by someone else (whether on videotape, audiotape, etc.) and that way your integrity will never be compromised.

In my experience, most officers are honest, honorable and intelligent people. But they don't enjoy writing, especially writing police reports. So sometimes the description of events reads more like a doctor's chart than a public document; descriptions are sometimes brief and littered with abbreviations that only a law enforcement officer can define. I've also read many incomplete police reports; boxes that ask for suspect/victim occupation, address, telephone number, driver's license number, etc. are often left blank. If the victim/suspect cannot provide this information at the time of the incident, the officer should consider making some sort of notation in the box (e.g. not available, no job, no address/homeless). Leaving a box blank is like writing an incomplete sentence, mysteriously ending after the verb. From the reporter's perspective, more information is almost always better than less.

I've included the suggestions that would be most helpful to me (and presumably other journalists too). Please accept these comments as they're intended: constructive, not critical.

Happy writing.

Solution to puzzle on page 15, ch. 2.

Technical Table of Contents